Bitcoin

or

Death

M. Haslem

Bitcoin or Death

Publisher: Bicycle For The Mind
ISBN: 978-0-6452712-7-0

Edition/Version 1.0
Lifetime updates for all customers will be
provided in a digital format. Visit bitcoinordeath.com/version
for the latest version number & details on how to get it.

DISCLAIMER: Not Financial Advice

The content provided in this book and associated materials is for entertainment purposes only. It is not intended as financial advice, life advice, or any advice what so ever, and should not be construed as such. Readers are encouraged to conduct their own research and consult with appropriate professionals before making any investment decisions, life decisions, or any decision what so ever. The author and publisher disclaim any liability for actions taken based on the content of this book.

Bonus Chapter

No matter your occupation, the question you'll face is: Bitcoin or Death?

Whether it's losing customers, risking your job, or jeopardizing your business, history shows that those who cling to a dying currency wither along with it.

This bonus chapter is crafted specifically to your occupation, illustrating how adopting Bitcoin could be your key to growth and a lifeline amidst a failing system.

Don't hesitate; unlock your industry-specific knowledge at:

BitcoinOrDeath.com/Bonus

The bonus is free, the only request: Share the book with 2 friends using the simple share buttons

From the Author

"Bitcoin or Death?"

...there's not much wiggle room with your options.

Dramatic? You bet. The question might seem absurd at first. Especially to those caught in the status quo, living in a system where the pain and destruction it leaves often goes unnoticed. But for those who have delved into the pages of history, who understand the atrocities that have transpired and know what's coming, this question transcends drama. It is a question that requires collective contemplation, one which we must all answer together, but ultimately a question that begins with you.

By the end of our journey, I will revisit this question with you. As your understanding deepens, you won't merely embrace the question; you'll become its advocate. You'll pose it daily to your friends, family, and loved ones - as casually as 'Coffee or tea?', 'Jeans or shorts?'...
Bitcoin or death?

Teaching others about Bitcoin: the process commonly referred to as "orange pilling," can be a hard pill for your friends to swallow. It requires NOT ranting about Bitcoin, but instead having them think about the current system, with all its flaws. It requires posing a question so direct that it stirs unavoidable thoughts.

For me, I started my orange pilling with a slow, deliberate approach. I wrote a fiction series, called "Generational Code," following an Apollo 11 engineer who dreamed of going to the moon. The books allowed readers to gradually absorb the ideas behind Bitcoin.

While fiction can be powerful, the time has come for a frank, open dialogue about whether we choose Bitcoin or remain within the current system. As humanity stands at the crossroads, our choice will determine if we forge a new path of hope, or repeat history and crumble into oblivion.

If my fiction books were a gradual orange pilling, a light dusting over the cereal, this book takes a more direct approach with a question you can't ignore...

Go to: BitcoinOrDeath.com And ask everyone you care about the hard question we all must confront.

At the site, you can pick up gift copies. For those reading this on an eBook, consider this a friendly nudge to embrace the physical copy too. There's a unique connection that forms when you physically interact with the question posed, and the commitment aspect alone becomes a tangible reminder of the choices you make.

Lastly, I want to express my heartfelt thanks for supporting my work! When it comes to getting the word out, reviews really make a difference, so if you enjoy the unique stories tucked away in the pages, I hope you can spare a moment to leave a review. Thanks so much for considering it, and I truly appreciate your support!

Going forth, this book will lay out the current system, as in what we've had for thousands of years, and then it will offer up an alternative and a challenge! The time for subtilty has passed. You now face one unavoidable choice: Bitcoin or Death?

CONTENTS

Death

Death is where we begin. To grasp the significance of Bitcoin and the birth of this new currency, it's essential to comprehend the system it aims to replace... what I refer to as "the Death."

Surprisingly, many struggle to describe the current financial system and thus associating it with the word "death" is far from their mind. But why does understanding evade so many?

For starters, it is complex by design. That's why, in this book, the complexities will be made clear; coupled with anecdotes, imagery and far from the Standard heavy reading.

But the complexity isn't entirely why we don't understand. The major reason is actually simple - immersion breeds ignorance. Like a fish unaware of the water it swims in, we are submerged in this system from birth. Its foundations shape our lives, its rules limit our choices. But rarely do we stop to question what we take for granted.

Alternatives appear inconceivable, so absolute is the status quo. We navigate our daily lives, seldom raising the question this book presents. However, history reminds us that nothing lasts forever, and perhaps it's time we shine a light on the remnants of past currencies, their lifeless skulls holding valuable historic lessons. The moment has come to re-examine our unwavering faith in our financial system we live.

And that faith starts early. When your schooling, your work and your media all revolves around the one system, it's all you know. It’s like asking a 2D Mario on the NES to fathom the vast dimensions of his 3D counterpart on the N64. For he has only ever known up, down, left and right – keep moving forward, collect the coins, level up, rescue the princess... we struggle to imagine anything beyond the rigid dimensions we inhabit.

To question the bounds of our financial universe provokes more than raised eyebrows - it elicits visceral defiance from those reliant on it. Incumbents and prisoners of the current system vehemently defend their captor, even as the cracks widen and the ground crumbles all around.

With that said, let’s now embark on a journey into the financial system that surrounds us. We'll explore its intricacies and its implications, and come to an understanding of the prevailing status quo — the world that Bitcoin challenges. The death.

Chapter 1 -
What the F*ck is Money?

Dazed and delirious, with the sun beating down, the only comfort I had was a slab of salt leaning against my leg. The desert had reduced me to a mere shadow, a fading echo of the man I once was. Sweat rolled down my forehead, the taste on my lips mirrored the very thing that was both my saviour and tormentor — salt.

With each laboured breath, I urged my faithful steed forward, our destination in sight. The distant village promised salvation in the form of water, sustenance, and rest. As we approached the marketplace, the harsh reality of my situation became painfully clear.

The villagers gathered around me, their eyes filled with longing as they saw the salt. It was more than a commodity; it was life itself in this unforgiving land. I knew the value it held would secure my survival, and so the bartering began.

Stories like this will transport us back to a time and place, in which each chapter will come alive, and we'll be thrown head first into the chaos together.

To live up to the title of this book, the questions posed and the discoveries uncovered, must be experienced, as if your LIFE depends on it!

Bitcoins greatest gift is compelling us to dig deeper, questioning assumptions we take for granted.

So, sit up, perch yourself on the edge of your chair, as we traverse this mental terrain, and ask the questions...

And what better place to start than with, "what is money?"

The concept of money has evolved over the ages. To this man living around 400 BC, salt was his currency. The term "salary" finding its roots in the Latin word "salarium," denoting payment to Roman soldiers for the purchase of salt.

At its simplest, money acts as a store of your work and effort. If you do 5 hours of work, you need something which will hold that value, until such a time in which you wish to spend it.

Throughout history, an array of items have played the role of money, from livestock and tablets to shells and coins. They have all taken on various forms to help elicit exchange.

In reality, nearly anything can serve as a form of currency, but not everything will endure, prove practical, or have lasting value. To assess whether what you possess qualifies as money and how effectively it functions as such, we can subject it to a set of criteria that define the properties of money.

The SIX properties of money:

1. Medium of Exchange: Money serves as a means of transacting, in a usually acceptable method. It acts as a way to pay for goods and services.

2. Durable: Money should have the ability to withstand wear and tear over time, ensuring it remains in circulation without deteriorating easily.

3. Divisible: Money should be divisible into smaller units, allowing it to represent values of various sizes and making it practical for both small and large transactions.

4. Portable: Money should be easily transported and transferred. It should have a physical form (e.g. cash or coins) or a digital representation (e.g. digital currency) that can be conveniently moved and used in various transactions.

5. Scarce: Money should be relatively scarce, meaning its supply is limited and cannot be easily created or inflated. This scarcity helps maintain its value over time.

6. Fungibility: Each unit of currency should be interchangeable and identical in value. It shouldn't matter where a specific unit of money comes from; they should all be the same and usable interchangeably in transactions.

Using this criterion to assess what you have in your wallet, purse, or account, should immediately raise some alarm bells, especially concerning money property #5. What you have instead is a currency, not money…

To be money, it must scarce and thus not easily eroded away. That's not to say, the stuff in our wallet didn't once hold significant value…

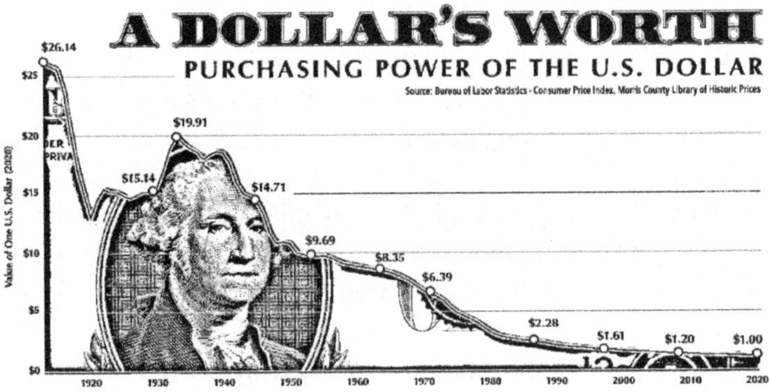

There was a time when those paper notes actually meant something. Not that long ago, our money carried weight, value and integrity. Printed notes weren't just a flimsy promise, at risk of losing value; but instead represented a physical claim.

Each bill served as an IOU from the issuing bank, redeemable for a specific amount of gold or silver. This connection made it challenging to manipulate, by anchoring the money to precious metals securely stored in vaults. For every dollar note that was issued, a dollar worth of gold would have to exist at the bank.

The notes being currency, the gold being money.

Why tie the dollar to gold? The answer is straightforward — gold excels as a store of value; having first been used by the Egyptians, it's maintained its purchasing power over the last 5000 years.

A paper currency tied directly to this valuable money, was a match made in heaven. But eventually, human nature kicked in, leading to actions that would disrupt this once harmonious union. As the Great Depression bought economic challenges, the US was taken off the gold standard by President Roosevelt in 1934, through the implementation of the Gold Reserve Act. This move granted the government the authority to issue more paper currency, without the necessity of an equivalent increase in gold reserves.

Although the dollar remained loosely tied to gold until the Vietnam War, Nixon's crucial decision to completely suspend the gold standard wasn't solely about funding the war. The U.S. had lent more notes than its gold reserves could cover. Countries were demanding their gold, and with reserves dwindling, a collapse was imminent.

While Nixon's decision may have averted crisis in the short term, it severed the last connection between paper currency and tangible money - setting us adrift without an anchor, supported only by hope — a true 'fiat currency.'

The word 'fiat' being derived from Latin, meaning 'let it be done' and as such, in shedding this constraint, the money lost its way. The last tie between paper and metals was severed, leaving value adrift without an anchor. Detached from tangible assets, new money could be conjured from thin air.

And so the presses ran hot, unbridled by former checks. Our wallets now held notes backed by nothing but hollow promises and growing debts. No longer fulfilling the definition of "money" as defined by our 6 principals, this strange new currency seemed one step removed from fantasy - conjured digits in a Federal Reserve database.

Our dollars may still say 'In God We Trust,' but the god is now the Fed. Their doctrine of inflation eroding our wealth, benefiting only those who hold assets in the inflated prices. Today's currency pays tribute to central bankers and the elite, not the precious metals that once shined so true for all.

So what path is the dollar on? When we look at history, we see that thousands of 'fiat' currencies have existed in the past, and they've all shared the same common destiny — being worth no more than the paper they were printed on.

Crazy right? Literally every single one has gone to zero.

You may not reside in the United States, but it's likely that your currency is also fiat-based, backed by nothing more than the same empty promises.

And since the US currency serves as a world reserve currency, nations that anchor themselves to it, find themselves subject to external influences beyond their control.

This isn't a theory or financial advice; nor is this book. Instead, it's a grand historical adventure we will embark on together, and perhaps, if we're lucky enough to rise above the confusion and distractions, we'll catch the faintest glimpse of a future beyond our wildest imaginations - a future that should have always been ours.

Like many of you, I learned what money is (and what it is NOT) from an unlikely crew. A ragtag bunch. Robert Kiyosaki, Max Keiser, Martin North, Mike Maloney AND ...Satoshi Nakamoto.

Why did I choose to learn from such an unconventional crew? Because the truth about money isn't found in the halls of Ivy League schools, on the news, or in the chambers of Congress. These sources often profit from the current system and may not provide an unbiased perspective.

Yes, to understand what Bitcoin is, we must first understand what it's looking to replace, what flaws the current system has...

"GET THE F*CK OUT OF THE WAY!" People rushed past me, shoving each other to get closer to the commotion. I was caught up in the frenzy, trying to see what was going on by the water's edge. The beach was a chaotic scene, with excited voices, waving hands, and the desperate determination of my fellow villagers.

A man, a stranger to our shores, stood by a boat loaded with seashells. He had a self-assured grin as he examined the goods being offered by my neighbours. "Two of these, three of those, and I'll take all of these," he declared, with an air of authority that demanded compliance. The people around hurried to fulfil his requests.

I gazed in awe at the spectacle unfolding before me. Bill gave me a nudge, "we're going to be rich, c'mon!" He took off in a dash towards the man; I followed behind.

"Here, bowls, wooden bowls," Bill pushed towards the front, his teetering hand-crafted goods flying left and right, one coming down right on my head. As I rubbed it off, the question lingered in my mind, how could this one man have amassed such wealth?

As he continued his extravagant purchases, more and more leaped onto his boat, eager to trade their possessions for his valuable seashells.

The villagers cheered while trying to keep up with his demands, as shells got passed around all over the place.

One landed by my feet, a beautiful specimen, which I picked up, feeling it over. "I'll be back with more," he said. "I want, everything!"

Others, who had boats at their disposal, hurried to prepare their vessels, determined to follow him and uncover the source of his wealth.

The next morning, our paradise had turned into a nightmare. The stable economy we had always known was unravelling, and the community was being torn apart by greed and desperation. In the midst of the destruction, I realized that the man's sudden wealth had come at a great cost. Our island, once peaceful and harmonious, was now marred by strife and uncertainty.

The issue with the shells was, they were not intrinsically scarce. Once someone rocked up on the island, and knew where to get extra shells, the supply was flooded, making everyone else's shells far less valuable.

As we've already discussed, the past hasn't always been doom and gloom. There's been a bright and enduring solution to money — an option that has maintained its value, outlasting its alternatives. Hyperbole aside, it's truly 'out of this world.'

It's shiny, hard to get, and it's been a store of value to those smart enough to hold it, especially through turbulent times... I'm talking about "God's money," sent from the heavens: precious gold.

We know gold didn't exist on Earth when our planet formed. Close to the surface, it's accessible through mining. In my home country, the ground can be so hard that gold is sometimes even found lying on the very top. If gold were here from the start, being a heavy metal, it would have sunk to the core when Earth was molten.

So how did it arrive here?

Exploding star. Gold, quite literally a product of exploding stars, journeyed through space and showered down from the heavens, scattering our planet with this precious metal.

So how did gold achieve this remarkable feat of maintaining its value over time? It all comes down to scarcity.

Among the six principles of money, scarcity should be given extra weight, as the other properties, such as divisibility and portability, lose their significance if its value has already eroded.

Obtaining gold is a laborious process that demands immense effort. This investment of time and toil, in a way, is reflected in the value it represents. Moreover, the slow rate of new gold discovery and extraction ensures that the inflation of available gold is gradual enough to prevent a rapid loss of its value.

What are the potential flaws in gold? The most obvious is its portability... of course, depending on your wealth. But remember, you don't always need to carry all your wealth at once. And if for this one flaw, you decide to be 100% balls-deep in your local 'shit-coin' currency, the convenience comes with a major flaw — all fiat has historically gone to zero.

Furthermore, while gold has been a remarkably reliable store of value, it has been abused in the past. The influence of 'paper gold' manipulation, unchecked issuance, and government seizures has prevented it from achieving the status of a 100% perfect form of money.

Looking ahead, the future of gold remains uncertain. With the potential for asteroid mining on the horizon, even the scarcity of gold could come into question. Although this concern may extend beyond our lifetimes, there exists the possibility that gold could once again descend from the heavens.

Irrespective of the form money takes, the historical tendency of human nature and centralized control to manipulate and devalue our money remains a constant challenge.

Chapter 2 -
Origins of Central Banks

As the last body fell on the blood-soaked battlefield, a lone messenger named Thomas spurred his horse into a frenzied gallop, the thundering hoofbeats echoing the chaos and carnage he'd just witnessed.

His mind raced with the gravity of the message he carried, a message that would alter the course of history. “I need to get to Nathan,” he muttered to himself as he approached the humongously regal door of the towering mansion.

Guarded and obstructed by burly gatekeepers, he thrust the crumpled dispatch into their hands, a mixture of determination and anger flashing in his eyes. They hesitated, then finally granted him passage.

Down the opulent hallway he raced, the scroll clenched tightly in his trembling hand, until he reached the grand chamber. Nathan Mayer Rothschild, a man of immense wealth and influence, stood expectantly. As Thomas handed over the sealed message, a triumphant smile slowly spread across Rothchild’s face, revealing the anticipation that had been building within him.

"Sell everything," Rothschild said with quite certainty. He now knew that Napoleon had suffered defeat at Waterloo, but he would use this inside knowledge for immense illicit gain.

Rothschild began selling his British bonds, engineering a market panic that sank their prices. This panic was just phase one of his ploy. Once prices crashed, Rothschild secretly bought the bonds back for pennies on the pound. When the public learned of Wellington's victory, bond prices skyrocketed. Rothschild emerged with enormous ill-gotten profits. His manipulation left the banks in shambles, forcing them to seek aid from none other than Rothschild himself.

In their desperation, the duped banks gave Rothschild unprecedented control to reshape Europe’s finances to his benefit. His deceitful ploy swindled the public, and he'd quite literally, through the bank's indebtedness, taken control of the Bank of England.

You see, control over central banks, or even acting as one, doesn't come about easily; it arises from crisis and ruins. The Rothschild's represented one of the earliest instances of formidable centralized power in the realm of banking, but to understand central banks, and their origins, we need to go further back, well before this battle of Waterloo...

Medieval banking practices were instrumental in shaping early monetary systems.

During this period, trade and commerce flourished in urban centres, and the need for secure storage and transfer of wealth became increasingly vital.

As trade expanded, the limitations of barter systems became apparent, leading to the development of commodity money. Items with intrinsic value, such as shells, salt, or precious metals, began to serve as mediums of exchange.

Goldsmiths, having established themselves as reliable guardians of precious metals, transitioned into financial intermediaries, issuing paper receipts as a representation of the wealth stored, an early form of promissory notes that would evolve into the concept of modern banknotes we have today.

This helped trade boom, as people could now exchange with

confidence, using a standardized form of currency, something which had fungibility, the sixth property of money.

This transition marked a crucial phase in the evolution towards more formalized banking structures, laying the foundation for the eventual establishment of central banks.

A central bank, these days, is responsible for far more than just issuing currency, it's pivotal in shaping the financial wellbeing of a nation.

The journey from the medieval goldsmiths to the establishment of central banks is a narrative of adaptation and evolution. As societies grew, trade flourished, and the need for a more sophisticated monetary system became apparent, laying the groundwork for what would become the cornerstone of modern finance.

In 1910, Across the Atlantic, on the secluded Jekyll Island, a covert plan was being hatched in the shadows.

A secret meeting to lay the groundwork for a powerful institution — USA's coveted central bank.

The population though, was not yet ready — they feared the concentration of power and dominance such a financial giant would wield.

But times were changing, banks were faltering, economies teetering on the brink of collapse. And the major opponents to it, had all just boarded a ship, a maiden voyage, of the Titanic. A ship partly owned by one of the want-to-be central bankers... JP Morgan.

"Iceberg ahead! The cry sent shivers down the spines of those aboard the grand ship, a marvel of its time, a symbol of opulence and progress. But beneath the gleaming façade lay a story far darker, where the whispers of power and wealth would converge at the crossroads of history.

As the Titanic met its fateful destiny in the icy abyss, a new colossal ship, be it on the financial stage, was now clear to set sail, ready to navigate the turbulent waters of change. The opposition lay silenced, and the Federal Reserve now loomed on the horizon, casting its shadow over the future.

Conspiracies aside, the public shock of Titanic's disaster not only marked a poignant moment in history but also played a role in distracting attention and shifting sentiment at a crucial juncture, as the Federal Reserve was approved. As it goes, crisis provided the opportunity for control, and the sinking of the Titanic created a distraction that allowed the architects of the Federal Reserve to seize greater authority during a time of upheaval.

As we move forward in this exploration of the modern financial system, remember that the echoes of history have a profound impact on the present system. A system whose centralized nature should be a concern to all.

Chapter 3 -
Centralization and Financial Control...

In a penthouse suite overlooking a glittering New York City, Henry Ford was not drawn to the roaring nightlife. Instead, he was immersed in a collection of books, seeking to unravel a well-guarded secret—one that even his wealth and stature could not grant access to.

As the clock neared midnight, Ford was on the verge of understanding. Each revelation quickened his pulse, and as the new year was met with fireworks and cheers, he turned to his confidant and declared, "It is well enough that people of the nation do not understand our banking and monetary system, for if they did, I believe there would be a revolution before tomorrow morning."

Henry Ford's midnight revelation about the monetary system ignited a scrutiny that continues to burn brightly today, captivating a population still as mystified by the veil of secrecy he once confronted.

Such secrecy and concern is synonymous with central banks. Central banks profess to champion the economic interests of nations, but their true motives often come into question. Beyond their grandiose claims of price stability and financial system protection, critics argue that central banks primarily serve the interests of the financial elite.

The issue arises with the concentration of control and power. As Lord Acton famously warned, 'absolute power corrupts absolutely.' When power over millions is centralized to a select few, even those with the best intentions can eventually succumb to self-interest.

The hunger for power often prevails, causing even initially noble individuals to transform into versions of themselves driven by profit and influence. Throughout history, the inherit risk in centralized power, has been the seedbed of corruption.

Even if the corruption never occurs, the fact that it could occur, that the situation exists, in which complete trust in one or a small bunch of humans is required, is an issue.

This is not necessarily a criticism of humanity, but rather an observation on the inherent tendencies of human nature. History repeatedly teaches us that undue temptation, can invite unethical actions. Be it an individual leader losing touch with their constituents or a legislative body more focused on self-interest, these scenarios are emblematic of power's potential for corruption.

This phenomenon isn't confined to any specific sector or organization. Movements, institutions, and structures across a spectrum of domains, including education, fact-checking, tech organizations, religion, sports, and even your local book club, can all succumb to biases, leanings and unfair wielding of power.

In the financial system, several entities hold significant centralized control. They include:

Central Banks

The concept of central banking can be traced back to the establishment of the Bank of Sweden in 1668. Its primary purpose was to provide a safer place for the government to store its gold and silver reserves. Over time, central banks began to take on broader roles, including the issuance of currency, regulation of commercial banks, and the management of monetary policy.

The Rothschild banking dynasty, which spanned the 18th and 19th centuries, epitomized the role of central banking during that era. With brothers strategically positioned across Europe's financial centres, they wielded substantial control over international finance. Nations often relied on their loans, making them influential in shaping the economic destinies of entire governments. The Rothschilds' vast centralized authority demonstrated how a single family's financial leverage could steer global affairs.

Other pivotal institutions in the history of central banking include the Bank of England, founded in 1694, and the Federal Reserve in the United States, established in 1913. Additionally, notable central banks from around the world include The Bank of France, established in 1800, The Bank of Japan, founded in 1882, and The European Central Bank, established in 1998, which is responsible for monetary policy within the Euro area.

Today, central banks exist in most countries, and their influence has only grown. And while I won't delve into conspiracies of which central banks are owned by which private entities, individuals or old families, we will however focus on the significant control they wield over economic policies, financial stability and the people in which they profess to be for.

IMF

Today, the International Monetary Fund (IMF) exerts similar centralized power as the Rothschild's once did. While created to foster global financial cooperation, the IMF has drawn criticism for perpetuating debt dependence and hardship. Its austerity requirements frequently harm borrowers' economies, stability and freedoms. For instance, El Salvador's decision to make Bitcoin legal tender in

September 2021 effectively led to the IMF withdrawing financing. Thus, even with stated good intentions, the IMF's centralized control over lending policies indulges a risky cycle of extending loans while compromising nations' self-determination.

Large Multinational Corporation

Beyond their financial power, large multinational corporations can also influence governments and policies through lobbying, campaign contributions, market power, and supply chain control. They often have a vested interest in shaping regulations and trade agreements to their advantage.

Private Equity and Venture Capital Firm

These entities have a substantial impact on the businesses and industries they invest in. Their decisions can influence the strategies and direction of companies and technologies that have far-reaching effects on the economy.

Credit Rating Agencies

Credit rating agencies wield significant influence by assigning ratings to various financial instruments. Investors heavily rely on these ratings, leading to substantial consequences when they are inaccurate, as seen in the 2008 global financial crisis.

Commercial banks

These institutions have a substantial impact on the businesses and industries they engage with, particularly when they partake in risky lending and investment practices which also contributed towards the 2008 GFC.

Now that we've covered some of the groups in which financial control has centralized around, lets focus on the most powerful: the Central Bank, and how they exert control today.

Central banks tweak levers of capital, credit, and liquidity availability, and their impact has grown enormously in recent decades with minimal oversight.

Interest rate policies represent the height of their power, allowing them to incentivize borrowing that now far exceeds productive capacity.

To control this interest rate, the central bank alters the 'basket of goods' in which inflation is calculated. This grants them license to constantly recalibrate, and as such, guiding rates down artificially. Critics expose this as a bald-faced suppression... the "CPLie" as it's known amongst the monetary circles of distrust.

And what's the significance of controlling the interest rate? This is where it all leads to, where the curtain lifts, and the grand show is revealed. With the ability to manipulate the interest rate, you can directly control the money supply.

The power to influence the cost of borrowing and lending is

a magic wand in the hands of central bankers. This power to print money—albeit indirectly — is at the heart of a system that may have been built with noble intentions, but over time, with human nature, it has been wielded in ways that benefit an elite minority.

With persistent low interest rates and unchecked stimulus, the repercussions of inequality, asset bubbles, and soaring personal debt have surged.

The epitome of centralized control is evident in the aftermath of the 2008 crisis, where the perpetrators went unpunished, while ordinary citizens bore the brunt of the economic catastrophe.

The crisis was but a tremor, yet in the absence of accountability and taxpayer-funded bailouts to save the day, it only guarantees further tremors and ultimately larger quakes.

A perpetual cycle where gains are privatized for banks and risks are systematically shifted onto the public.

Beyond just Wall Street, main street bore the brunt of the GFC through business closures, lost jobs, and evaporated savings. The crisis turbocharged wealth inequality and deepened the social divide. Mental health deteriorated under the strains of financial pressure, while homelessness swelled in cities across the country.

Yet even as millions struggled, elite circles escaped unscathed, insulated by the very system that caused such pain.

While the crisis was an extreme manifestation, the societal implications persist in milder forms today. Opaque central bank policies like rampant quantitative easing continue entrenching inequality and inflation while failing to meaningfully benefit those most vulnerable.

Until wrongdoers face dire repercussions, history will repeat in this rigged system that concentrates power and protection at the top.

The solution and ultimate answer to escape this pain, would be to not centralize power in the first place. This way, the potential bait leading to corruption is never dangled. Sadly, that can never exist.

Or can it...? Some good DID come out of the 2008 financial crisis, one which may just solve the centralized problem, ripping the power from those who abuse it most.

While control is often centralized among a select few power brokers, true power ultimately rests with the collective will of the people. When pushed to such breaking points, such as the GFC, the pain acts as a catalyst for true change and mass awakening. Henry Ford's midnight epiphany, 'a revolution before tomorrow morning,' may have already arrived and a financial revolution could very well be underway.

Chapter 4 -
The Theft of Wealth

"More, more! Add it in!" his voice boomed through the opulent chambers of the ancient city. In the dimly lit mint, a fateful transformation was underway. The silver denarii, a symbol of Roman might, was being ruthlessly altered.

With each addition of copper, the very essence of the silver coin was changing. What once gleamed with purity, now bore the mark of the emperor's decision that would echo through history.

As the mint's craftsmen complied with Nero's orders, subtle murmurs of dissent and despair permeated the air. One worker, feeling the weight of the debasement, couldn't help but murmur, "But Sir, people are commenting on your nose." Nero lifted his hands to his face. "No Sir, your nose on the coin, it's rubbing off in their pockets." The worker held out a coin, its surface worn, leaving Nero red-nosed, the copper beneath peeking through; a symbol of its decline mirroring the empire's downfall, and altering the world's understanding of currency forever.

Just like with the newly found shells, Nero had debased the currency in which Rome relied on. He'd siphoned away the coins rare silver value, by mixing in abundant and worthless copper. This was to fast-track coin production for funding their ever-expanding empire and wars. Sound familiar?

The debasing of the coins became even more evident to the people, when taxes subsequently were demanded in the original silver coins, showcasing to everyone that clearly not even the government valued their newly minted coins.

These days, debasing the money supply is done with fancy names. They call it MMT.

...What's that acronym?

Oh don't you worry
...C'mon, what is it?

"Modern Monetary Theory"... you see the stuff in the past didn't work, because they were stupid... Nero's an idiot... We are much smarter now, this won't end as all the other fiats have, this is modern... don't you want to be modern?

Let's first take a look at how much the money supply has ballooned within the US as of late:

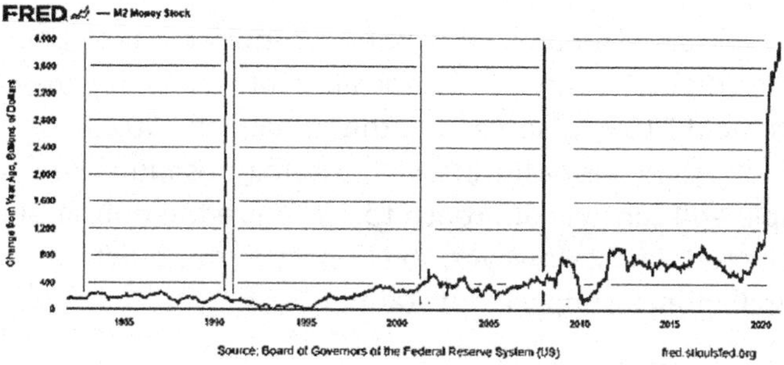

This is the M2 money supply in the US, but it could just as easily be a chart of Rome's coin minting, towards the end of its empire. M2 is a measure of how much money is in the system... it includes all physical currency like coins and paper money but also various types of deposits in financial institutions, such as banks and credit unions.

And it's not just the USA — look up the 'money supply chart' of your own country, whether you're in Australia, Canada, India, China... nearly every country has been doing massive deficit spending and increasing their money supplies over the past few decades.

So how did it get like this? Let's look at the major vehicles the central banks have used to increase the money supply...

Fractional Reserve Lending

A complex system where banks are required to hold only a fraction of the deposits they receive as reserves, typically a small percentage, while they can lend out the rest to borrowers. This fraction is known as the reserve requirement.

For example, if a bank has a reserve requirement of 10%, it means that for every $100 deposited into the bank, they must hold $10 in reserve, and the remaining $90 can be lent out to individuals or businesses. This might sound like a simple and sensible approach to maximize the utilization of deposited funds. However, the impact of this practice on the overall money supply is substantial.

When a bank lends out the $90 from the example above, it enters the economy as a new loan. Let's say this money is borrowed to buy a car. The borrower, in turn, pays the car seller, who deposits the money into another bank. That bank, following the same reserve requirement, holds a fraction of this deposit as a reserve (let's say $9) and lends out the rest ($81). This process repeats as new loans are made and funds are deposited.

As this cycle continues, it results in what is known as the "money multiplier effect." The initial $100 deposit has now led to a much larger sum circulating in the economy, far beyond the original deposit. This means that every new loan essentially creates new money within the banking system.

The banks are lending out money, they don't even have! This increased money supply contributes to both economic expansion and the devaluation of the currency.

Quantitative Easing

A modern twist to the age-old practice of debasing currency. It involves a central bank purchasing government securities or various financial assets from the market with the intention of injecting new money into the economy. While this approach is aimed at stimulating short-term economic growth and market stability, it can also have long-term inflationary effects. If we ourselves were to sit in our garages, and print money, we'd be in massive trouble with the law. It's illegal and it's unfair on all those holding legitimate money, as we've conjured ours out of thin air. Yet this is what Quantitative Easing is; they are essentially doing the same thing, but getting away with it. Their license to print, causes the devaluation of your money over time, diminishing your purchasing power.

Deficit spending

Governments often undertake substantial off-budget spending, especially during crises like pandemic responses and wars. These endeavours, while we are told are crucial, are almost always funded through borrowing from other countries. For instance, pandemic responses witness massive spending on healthcare, stimulus packages, and other measures to combat the crisis. The costs of wars, including military operations, infrastructure rebuilding, and veterans' benefits, also contribute to the accumulation of debt. Repaying this debt often involves printing more money, further impacting the money supply and, consequently, ramping up inflation.

The terms may have changed, but the act remains, history repeats, and the outcome is the same... they are effectively putting copper in the coins! These practices, with their fancy names, can quite simply be understood by our own poetic term, *money go brrrr*

The issue with the money printing, as was in Rome, and common amongst the end cycle of all great empires, is the money becomes worth less. Worthless, worth-less... the two words going hand in hand, first being worth less, then ultimately, it's worthless.

With an inflated supply, your purchasing power is eroding. While some will call it "cost of living" and try to explain it away by saying "things are just naturally get more expensive", or "businesses are getting greedy," or better yet, they'll come up with reasons while each individual item has increased in price... a shortage of strawberries in the North, the bananas were affected by the floods, the shipping has slowed tomatoes, covid is to blame for expensive cars... know all too well that it's as simple as copper getting added to the coins.

It's not that the items have suddenly all gone up in price; it's the very money you price things in, is getting less valuable. Your money is being debased, your money is losing its power, your money is being stolen from right under your nose.

To add fuel to this fire, as inflation is so often misunderstood or manipulated, governments will increase rates, to “combat” the inflation. They will act like they don’t know where the inflation came from, that they didn’t see it coming, that it caught them off guard. But what they will be certain of is their response. Pumping interest rates to “fight” this sudden unforeseen inflation, is the ultimate 1-2 punch for the citizens, as everything they buy is more expensive, and now all their loans are also more costly.

One man who understands it, musician and rapper 50 cent, eloquently put it like this:
“I don't want to be 20cent”

The fact is, as it always has been for fiat currency — as the supply is increased, people’s wealth is devalued.

If the money supply drastically doubles, within a three-year period...

- Someone who has worked hard and saved diligently their entire life, has essentially lost half of their purchasing power. Or more accurately, they have had half of their wealth stolen.

- If you get paid in the currency that’s being printed, you’ve essentially had half of your wage stolen.

- If you hold superannuation, it’s essentially been cut in half... half your money for retirement has been stolen.

- If you are on a fixed income, such as a pension, you’ve had half of your pension stolen.

- If you run a small business, your operational costs... your rent, your power, has all doubled... and your dreams have potentially been stolen.

You see, inflation steals far more than dollars; it robs us of time, labor, and the true rewards of our efforts.

Some refer to it as a “hidden tax” on the population, effectively reducing people's purchasing power and savings without their consent. It’s something that we really had little to no say over, and yet it happens all the time.

By expanding the money supply, the government silently picks the pockets of hardworking people. It is an insidious, unlegislated tax inflicted without consent. This pilfering of wealth hits vulnerable populations hardest - fixed income seniors, wage workers, small business owners, savers. Those least able to protect themselves suffer the most. It is a moral outrage, a breach of public trust at the highest levels.

Officials have a sacred duty to promote the general welfare, yet this hidden tax flies in the face of that duty. Innocent people's quality of life and financial security are being stolen as they sleep, while the powerful elite hoard the newly created money and their assets appreciate.

Yes, those with assets that are priced in the inflated currency, not only weather the storm the best, they can benefit from it. Home owners, stocks owners, holders of precious metals, and more can find themselves benefiting from the money printing, as there is now more money in the system, and the price of their hard assets have been inflated along with the money supply.

Thus, it's at the behest of this elite group, to divert your attention away from what's happening. To steer your focus in the wrong direction. To have the news report on individual item costs; like the cost of petrol, the price of lemons, or a carton of eggs... always avoiding the real issue, never discussing the currency itself, never addressing the root cause, and never acknowledging the printing.

Being a hidden tax, especially when it occurs gradually, people often fail to notice it initially. The cost of living quietly and steadily climbs, making everyday life more challenging. Yet, like a frog in a pot of slowly boiling water, we become desensitized to these changes, barely recognizing the impact, while the distractions orchestrated by the elite divert our attention. We tend to blame individual products, companies, and even local mom-and-pop businesses for raising their prices.

If inflation continues unabated, we risk facing an economic catastrophe. Just as in Rome, hyperinflation could trigger complete financial collapse. Savings could become worthless overnight. Retirements built over decades washed away in a sea of money printing. Prices will spin out of control, necessities unattainable. Faith in institutions may erode. Social unrest, even violence could ensue as citizens realize their labor and assets were stealthily stripped away. We could see a full restructuring of economic systems, mass poverty, and loss of stability.

The very fate of our nation hangs in the balance if those in power do not alter course. But for now, it goes unnoticed.

The squeeze is felt, the hidden tax is paid, and the wealth is stolen from under our feet. By the time realization dawns, it'll be too late; for most have not reached the point of awareness that matters, most are not yet ready to stand up and say, "Hey Nero, stop!"

Chapter 5 -

Endless Wars: How Fiat Fuels Conflict

The weight of my helmet bore down on my forehead, discomfort gnawing at me as I trudged along the cobbled path. "Hurry the f*ck up," the commander's voice echoed down the line, but I was falling behind, once more.

It felt like an endless cycle. When would I get a moment to myself, to catch my breath? When could I sit, to relax my legs? When could I rest... like my fallen comrades? If Rome were to collapse, I thought, at least I'd find peace amongst them.

A common theme with fiat currency is war. They go hand in hand: war requiring funds, funds requiring war. This happens, for war is costly to finance, but war is also profitable.

Costly for a nation and its citizens to fund; from a human toll standpoint, as well as monetarily. But at the same time, profitable for those invested in it. With military stocks, supply contracts, destroying and rebuilding...

> *"The goal is to use war to wash money out of the tax bases and into the hands of transnationals security elite. That is the goal. The goal is to have an endless war, not a successful war. We have to prevent it becoming normal, for there to be a constant war."*
>
> \- Julian Assange

When profiteering from conflict exists, the drums of war will inevitably sound. Its beat propelling more bright-eyed youths to the slaughter and more lucrative agreements to eager profiteers.

In the corridors of power, there exists a strong relationship between the military-industrial complex, a network of defence contractors, and the financial elite. They exert tremendous influence over the decision to wage wars. These entities have a vested interest in conflict, as it drives demand for their products and services.

The allure of war-time profits casts a long shadow over the decisions made in the halls of government, where interests often conflict with the will of the people. The potential for financial gain not only affects the choice of going to war but also the duration and scale of conflicts.

Governments have a well-practiced art of manipulating public sentiment, particularly when it comes to justifying military actions. Government propaganda can shape public opinion, often through fear, nationalism, and the portrayal of war as a necessary evil. Often it won't even be labelled war; but positioned as aid, protecting our partners, or defending democracy, as it's a much easier sell.

Whatever the term, by framing war as essential, governments work hand in hand with the media, to rally support from their citizens. The public, unaware of the hidden costs and monetary expansion required to fund it, inadvertently perpetuates the cycle.

With the public now onboard, where exactly does the money come from to fill the governments war chest?

Central banks and governments maintain a cozy relationship, enabling the constant state of endless wars. By acting as a ready purchaser of government debt, central banks provide the easy money needed to fund military adventurism. This harmonious partnership, marching in lockstep, removes spending discipline and allows conflicts to drag on.

With central banks willing to monetize deficits, governments feel minimal pressure to balance budgets or resolve wars quickly. The resulting monetary expansion then breeds economic instability and devalued currency, perversely incentivizing even more military conquests abroad.

And thus, the trajectory of endless military endeavours becomes an unfortunate certainty. Money feeding war, war feeding money.

Bankers on the other hand, get first dibs on the new currency, enriching themselves through privileged access. Politicians channelling the funds to their allies and military campaigns, secure lobbying money and strengthen their own political power, ensuring they remain in their roles. And the elite benefit with prices of their hard assets inflating. But it is the ordinary citizens who ultimately bear the cost.

And pay they do, in blood and treasure. An endless cycle, as long as the war drums drown out their cries, new money pours in, perpetuating the system and enabling ever greater conflicts.

The immense sums spent on endless wars and military interventions carry a great opportunity cost. As trillions are funnelled into the war machine, critical domestic priorities go chronically underfunded. Healthcare, education, infrastructure, and social welfare programs suffer from lack of investment. Consider the over $6 trillion spent on the 'War on Terror' since 2001. Imagine if even a fraction of that funding had gone towards healthcare research, rebuilding crumbling bridges and roads, or supporting programs to lift citizens out of poverty.

When military spending dominates budgets, urgent human needs get neglected. Funds that could have improved lives and strengthened communities instead get deployed overseas in a quest for military supremacy. The opportunity cost of an endless war is a steep price paid by a nation's own people. Both their current hardship and lost potential must be reckoned with.

Channelling vast resources into military endeavours doesn't just fuel inflation through unchecked money printing; it also has a hidden impact through imposing huge demand on wartime purchases.

The giant surge in spending on military supplies, causes an increased demand for raw materials, triggering a domino effect across the economic spectrum. As military entities vie for an increasing share of these resources, the raw material prices soar, ultimately impacting a vast array of day-to-day consumer products.

Until the populace finally tunes out the incessant pounding, and listens to the stories of those who have truly paid the price, only then can the drumbeat of endless war be silenced.

The cycle of war though is no surprise, much like in Rome — war and money printing ramps into hyperdrive towards the end of an empire, each one fuelling the other, perpetuating the debt and pain.

The age-old saying of, "Good times create weak men," runs true, as empires prosper and enjoy periods of stability, they often become complacent, losing their discipline and resolve...

The desire for wealth and power fuels a cycle where governments overextend themselves, resorting to conflict and conquest...

To finance these ambitions, they resort to money printing, which, in turn, leads to economic instability and the erosion of the currency's value....

As history has shown, this pattern repeats, with the great powers always losing sight of the principles that once made them so strong.

For the Roman Empire, their wars had become so numerous, it was the fighting on multiple fronts and funding the machine which led to its eventual collapse.

Not all history repeats, but it often rhymes,
and the drums of war sync across empires, and throughout time.

The fallen know peace, a rest coming for all,
For being fiat based, is being for war.

Chapter 6 -
Fiat is Killing our Planet

My hands clamped the wheel, the sweat making it difficult to control the armoured beast. "Slow down!" my co-worker pleaded, his words barely audible over the roar of the engine tearing through the streets. Replenishing the thirsty money machines had become routine, but the stakes were rising.

As we neared the final ATM, a deafening explosion shattered the morning calm. Smoke and chaos erupted in the distance. The radio crackled with dispatch's panicked voice, "Turn back, it's too dangerous!" My chest tightened, but I didn't waver.

I stole a glance at my panicked companion, his trembling hand resting on his holstered gun. "We'll be okay," I declared, flooring the accelerator, "Keep the cash secure... this war isn't ours."

He nodded in agreement, though it was clear he didn't fully buy into my reassurance. The journey back was spent in tense silence, the echoes of war ringing in my ears...

It's quite rich when critics decry Bitcoin's energy use, while overlooking the negative impacts of the very system it looks to replace; one that bears a considerable toll on Mother Nature. Endless skyscrapers house swarms of paper-pushing bankers. Armoured trucks roar down highways, burning fuel merely to shuttle dollars from one location to another. Vast resources are wasted to maintain an illusion of efficiency in a broken system.

Part of this masquerade is done with so-called "green scoring." Massive investment firms wield them to coerce companies into maintaining the status quo. By threatening to withhold funds, they effectively blackmail corporations to toe the line on what they deem acceptable. This carefully-crafted PR masks the hidden ecological impacts lurking behind every fiat transaction.

Each banknote and digital dollar leaves a trail of devastation... from the forests felled to make paper bills, to the plastic cards fuelling a toxic waste crisis, our banking system is far from perfect. The supposed efficiency of modern finance versus Bitcoin, is a mirage, designed to keep profits flowing and scrutinizing questions at bay.

Those who believe humanity is destroying our planet, must look beyond Bitcoin to the system that spawned our current state of affairs. Bitcoin is relatively new; the root causes of environmental damage stretches back generations. Criticism centred on surface level details, not only miss the point, but are purposely disingenuous.

Comparing the ecological impact of mining rigs powering the Bitcoin network, to an ATM machine only begins to uncover the depth of the issue, as it's this sort of superficial analysis which becomes sensationalized fodder for mainstream media. Each article attacking Bitcoin over the years, is etched into the public record, forever cementing their stance in defending the very systems responsible for wreaking havoc on our planet.

To get to the bottom of the true ecological cost fiat has, we must take into account everything a fiat-based currency enables. Moving money is only the beginning, the very tip of the iceberg; the hidden toll on the environment remains obscured.

Fiat fuels mass production and waste, incentivizing planned obsolescence and superficial consumption. It subsidizes the destruction of natural habitats for resource extraction and urban sprawl. Worst of all, fiat propping up endless growth at all costs has birthed a culture blind to ecological consequences.

It's not just in commercial sectors - the effects of fiat extend into much darker corners... Wars made capable through fiat-based currency, inflict a devastating toll on our planet at various stages, from the battlegrounds to the production of machinery and weaponry.

Fighter jets, tanks and transportation... as the engines of destruction roar to life, entire cities are flattened and landscapes scarred, leaving a long-lasting imprint. From a contaminated future to complete ecosystems sacrificed at the altar of endless war, the planet bears the hidden costs.

The devastation spreads far beyond the immediate frontline locations. The astronomical energy and resources required for modern warfare bring heavy ecological consequences. Vast mining operations pummel the earth while extracting the raw materials needed for fuelling the endless conflicts. Oil-guzzling transport swarms across land and sea, delivering the materials to refineries and then production lines. At every step, the petroleum-powered war machine pollutes the atmosphere while ravaging landscapes to feed its ever-increasing appetite.

Rebuilding what has been destroyed only compounds the damage, as the cycle accelerates. Over and over, forests are razed to the ground, waters polluted, and communities uprooted; silent victims in the all-consuming march to war.

War profiteers and bankers benefitting from the currency printing, jet off to exotic getaways on carbon-spewing private planes. Money printing keep luxury yachts afloat and sprawling vacation homes thriving, emblems of opulence bankrolled by government military spending.

These symbols of excess are frequently funded by hard-earned taxpayer dollars, rewarding the very institutions responsible for damages to our planet.

The consequences of rampant money printing extend to all corners of the earth, even to those that have nothing to do with the waging wars.

As the United States continues to flood the world with its dollars, it inadvertently places tremendous strain on other countries, particularly those burdened with debts denominated in US currency. These nations find themselves caught in a relentless cycle - while the US prints more dollars for themselves, the smaller nations bear the weight of obligations that remain static in dollar terms, becoming increasingly difficult to repay.

Often faced with no choice, as their nations become poorer, they turn to dirtier, but more affordable forms of energy generation to power their country. The green initiatives they aspired to adopt become casualties of necessity. Pollution rises, environmental commitments wane, and the planet suffers the consequences.

With every "printer go brrr," the ecological toll compounds, underscoring the harsh reality that the fate of our planet is inexorably intertwined with the financial decisions made on a global scale.

The misaligned incentives and short-term thinking caused by unsound money, are the culprits of our current economic and environmental ills. Unless we trace our situation back to this root source, no solution can take hold. A legacy of unbacked currencies made this bed; now we must either lie in it, or build the foundations of a new system, with foresight for generations to come.

We can get mad, upset, and scream... but it will continue. As long as the financial system that profits from conflict remains, the planet will suffer. The fiat system will continue to silently subsidize environmental destruction.

As individuals, all we can do is take control of what lies within our power. Relying on fiat inadvertently contributes to environmental degradation on a sweeping scale, fuelling steel mills and carpet bombing the planet... and there's no amount of egg carton recycling or paper straws that will make up for that.

The planet's destruction isn't some distant phenomenon beyond our reach. It's right there in our pockets, sought after, and worked for. We drive the truck of fiat currency, the destruction in plain sight out the window. When we fully embrace the fiat-based system, we unwittingly become accomplices in the devastation of the natural world meant to sustain us all.

For being fiat-based, is being against Mother Nature.

Chapter 7 -
Fiat for ILLEGAL activity

Under the cover of night, a nondescript van pulled up to a bustling port. Its precious cargo - bundles of cash, bricks of powder, contraband destined for distant shores. The transaction was brief, the illicit goods quickly changing hands from traffickers to transporters.

As the van peeled away, a few stray $20 bills were caught in its wake, twisting helplessly in the night air before settling in the dirty gutter, the only remaining evidence of the illegal transaction.

Trillions of US dollar bills circulate worldwide, the currency of choice for illegal enterprises.

Here are just some specific examples of large-scale illegal activities that involve the use of fiat currency:

Money Laundering: Criminal organizations often launder their ill-gotten gains through banks and other financial institutions. Like Marty Byrde and Walter White, they take dirty money and run it through legitimate financial channels to make it appear clean. Banks have had to pay fines in the past, for turning a blind eye. There are many examples, here's one: "HSBC was fined $1.9 billion in 2012, for most notably, serving as a conduit for Mexican drug cartels."

Corruption and Bribes: Bent government officials involved in corruption, will often accept bribes directly in cash, making it difficult to trace or prove. These activities undermine trust in public institutions and hinder economic development.

Organized Crime: The world of organized crime relies heavily on paper cash. From extortion rackets to illegal gambling, many such activities are fuelled by fiat currency.

Tax Evasion: Individuals and corporations can evade taxes by dealing in cash, keeping transactions off the books. This costs government's significant revenue that could otherwise be used for public services.

Human Trafficking: Human trafficking networks often deal in cash transactions. Smugglers and human traffickers prefer cash to avoid traceability.

Illegal Arms Trade: The global arms trade involves vast sums of money. Arms dealers, who may operate illegally or covertly, frequently deal in cash, making their activities difficult to track.

Black Market Activities: Counterfeit goods, illegal drugs, and other black-market items are often bought and sold with cash. This underground economy operates outside the purview of the law.

Despite all of these examples, it's cryptocurrency that draws outrage from politicians and the media, who seem to work together, hand in hand, in an attempt to stifle adoption.

Just like the US Dollar, cryptocurrencies can facilitate illegal transactions. Money is essentially a medium of exchange, and it's important to recognize that blaming the currency itself is misguided. This is especially true when considering the extent to which the existing monetary system is intertwined with various criminal activities. Attempting to ban cryptocurrencies is akin to confiscating plastic knives while ignoring machetes.

The US dollar gets away Scott-free, evading scrutiny despite being the preferred currency of criminals, deeply entrenched within the underworld. Rather than pretend crypto is solely to blame and ignoring fiat's dark legacy, it may prove wiser to go after the actual wrongdoers responsible for the illicit actions.

Recently, Senator Bill Hagerty of the US congress challenged the "terror funding figures" related to cryptocurrency, as reported on by the Wall Street Journal. He points out that these figures are disputed, and according to independent analysis, the WSJ "numbers" could be overestimated by as much as 99%. This was determined through blockchain analysis, as the open nature of the public ledger, can bring mistruths to light.

It's this type of incorrect reporting, whether it be from incompetence, honest mistakes, or deliberate malpractice: that banks, governments and all those who look to ban or stifle adoption then run with.

Banks will use negative reporting as an excuse to block its users from sending money to crypto exchanges. They'll claim it's to protect their users, because "crypto" has been used by criminals in the past. The irony being, it's the same banks that have enabled epic scales of money laundering and organized crime in the past. The sheer velocity of illicit transactions facilitated by major financial institutions dwarfs any potential abuse of cryptocurrency.

What the banks won't say, at least out loud, that they are attempting to keep you within their system. If their claims were true, that they wanted to protect you from currencies that have been associated with crime in the past, then they would also prevent you from holding US Dollars, British Pounds, Euros, Australian Dollars...

Attempts by banks to hamstring its users who wish to opt out of their fiat-based systems and use alternatives, is usually 100% disingenuous, and while it might keep a small number of people safe, the trade-off is, the average citizen suffering from reduced freedoms.

The criminals will find ways around the laws and any restrictions will ultimately fail, as code crosses borders more freely than people or paper.

The bank users, which have been locked out from participating in something they have every right to do, will also find a way. When stopped by their bank, from sending their own money to a cryptocurrency exchange — the hardest money, as we see throughout history, will win.

People will eventually get paid directly in Bitcoin, they will hold the Bitcoin themselves, and they will use their Bitcoin for purchasing goods and services. They will completely make the banking system that shunned them, obsolete. They will be their own bank.

As the traditional financial system has willingly allowed illegal activities under the cover of night to thrive, their time is almost up, and the landscape is changing. People are discovering a new way to conduct transactions, free from the grip of banks and fiat currency. One day, they won't need the dirty, blood-soaked fiat-currency. One day, they will simply opt out.

Because being for fiat, is being for crime.

Chapter 8 -
Fiat & Religion

Determined to save his beloved church, Father Michael embarked on a mission to raise the necessary funds to replace the crumbling roof after his local Mayor backtracked on his funding promises.

While the church did have some savings put aside for maintenance, they were wholly unprepared for the exorbitant costs in today's economy.

Father Michael organized charity events, community gatherings, and his congregation came together, contributing what they could to help keep the church's doors open.

As the fundraising efforts slowly gained momentum, his hope was rekindled. He saw the power of collective action and the compassion of his community. But just when it seemed they might succeed, misfortune struck. The funds they had collected were stolen, leaving the church's future once again in jeopardy.

Father Michael's faith in humanity was shaken, yet he clung steadfastly to his beliefs. The stolen funds were a loss, but the one thing the thief could never take, were the values he himself lived by, etched in stone – the principles that guided him through life's trials and tribulations.

As fiat currency loses trust and a sense of faith in its stability wanes, a noticeable split in moral values between the world of finance and religion becomes increasingly evident.

'In God We Trust,' the motto intertwined with money's origin and its historical connection to religion, now seems far from its original intent in today's financial landscape.

Currency comes and goes; but principles and values are the only true stores of wealth. In this chapter, we delve into the interplay of these two realms, exploring the profound moral and ethical values rooted in religious teachings and their relevance to the modern financial landscape.

> Matthew 21:12-13 (NIV):
>
> *"Jesus entered the temple courts and drove out all who were buying and selling there.*
>
> *He overturned the tables of the money changers and the benches of those selling doves.*
>
> *'It is written,' he said to them, 'My house will be called a house of prayer, but you are making it a den of robbers.'"*

Within religious scripture, we find such values and principles that have guided humanity's moral compass throughout time; one of the biggest being, 'thou shall not steal.'

And it wasn't just Jesus and Christianity who were prepared to flip tables over upholding such morals. In Islam, theft is strictly forbidden and is considered a sin. The Quran, the holy book of Islam, contains verses that emphasize honesty and prohibit stealing. Hinduism, with its concept of dharma, underscores ethical and moral responsibilities... stealing is seen as a violation of one's dharma and is considered morally wrong. In Buddhism, which emphasizes ethical conduct and the principle of not harming others, clearly condemns stealing, as it contradicts these core principles. Sikhism, Judaism, and other major religions also promote honesty, respect for property, and an unequivocal prohibition against taking what does not rightfully belong to you. They all share a fundamental moral and ethical guideline against dishonesty and theft...

Living by this moral compass extends to the realm of currency and the financial systems that underpin modern societies, affirming that the money one earns should not be subject to covert confiscation or devaluation.

Unfortunately, this principle is tested daily in the world of central banks and fractional reserve lending. Through these mechanisms, the hard-earned savings of individuals are gradually diluted, effectively becoming an unseen tax and the theft of one's finances...

Yet it often goes unnoticed, with the inflation blamed on anything but the inflated money supply. Strikes, rising petrol prices, or necessary wars; all mental gymnastics, to avoid admitting the direct theft of the citizens purchasing power; the sin of fiat.

Fiat, by its very definition as government-issued legal tender, relies on faith in institutions for its worth. Without the backing of a hard asset, absolute trust is needed in the government, central banks and monetary policies. Yet these days, they all seemingly contradict moral principles, and are far removed from the values in which they were once built upon.

Trust is the real currency; when it's lost, no amount of money can compensate. As people are coming to this realisation, they are seeking new systems of value with foundations as steadfast as religious doctrine.

They seek a store of value that measures righteous work and deed, not unrestrained extravagance. The relationship between currency and religion has always been entangled, and as old paradigms falter, new paradigms are rising to fill the moral void.

For Father Michael, he eventually saved enough for the church's repairs, but it took much longer than expected, as he had to grapple with the cruel irony that the original price quoted had gone through the roof.

Chapter 9 -
Fiat's Hidden Chains

I hurriedly excused myself from the checkout line, the embarrassment weighing heavy on my shoulders. The cashier's empathetic smile couldn't disguise the frustration in her eyes. Clutching my bewildered child's hand, I stepped aside and took a deep breath.

In my wallet, the stack of credit cards resembled a disorganized deck of shuffled playing cards. Each one represented a different financial obligation, and I'd lost track long ago.

"One of these should have room," I muttered to myself, but it was wishful thinking at best. My financial juggling had reached the point where I was desperately trying to keep the plates from crashing to the ground, each card adding another link to the chain that bound me.

The cashier held my groceries, waiting patiently, while I made a hasty excuse, "I'll be back with cash." She didn't say a word, but her knowing look conveyed understanding. She could see through my flimsy lie. She glanced down at my child, whose innocent eyes were filled with curiosity and a hint of confusion. With a tender smile, she handed my kid an apple, a silent gesture of compassion, in the face of my financial death.

In the complexity of modern finance, one particularly dangerous snare often eludes our notice—the debt trap, a set of hidden chains that bind us. It lies in wait, concealed by a veil of economic intricacies, and yet its consequences can be profound and far-reaching. This chapter embarks on a journey into the heart of the debt trap, shedding light on how the complex web of financial obligations entrap individuals, businesses, and even entire nations.

Debt is the lifeblood of modern finance, coursing through the veins of economies worldwide. It can empower individuals to acquire homes, entrepreneurs to fund innovative ventures, and governments to sustain public services. However, this very financial tool can become a double-edged sword, cutting into the financial stability and well-being of those who wield it unwisely.

The debt trap enigma lies, in part, within the mechanisms that facilitate the relentless accumulation of debt...

In many other countries, banks and the government have actively encouraged the availability of cheap money, particularly in the context of home purchases. The housing market has become their cash cow, with ever-increasing house prices their primary goal. Some critics even argue that the various initiatives in place could be seen as market manipulation, as they work tirelessly to artificially inflate the prices. This focus on lending to buy houses comes at a cost, as it often takes precedence over lending to businesses, which are the real engines that drive economic growth and create jobs.

So instead of focusing where we should, we are focused on getting individuals into housing markets which are already pumped, meaning huge debt.

Personal Debt:

In the pursuit of life's aspirations, individuals turn to various financial instruments to fund their endeavours. Student loans grant us access to education, with the hopes of jobs at the end of it. Mortgages enable us to buy homes, credit cards offer convenience and immediate access to resources, and loans provide financial flexibility. While these financial tools serve as stepping stones to our goals, they can also become the stones that weigh us down in the debt trap.

The consequences of personal debt are profound, stretching beyond financial spreadsheets and bank statements. Indebtedness can cast a shadow over one's financial stability and well-being. It can lead to a cycle of repayments that consumes a substantial portion of income, reducing the capacity to save and invest in the future. It can also affect creditworthiness, influencing access to financial opportunities and even employment prospects.

Furthermore, the weight of personal debt takes a toll on emotional and psychological realms. The constant worry about repayments and the pressure of meeting financial commitments can erode mental well-being, strain relationships and lead to the feeling of being trapped in an unending cycle, with no light at the end of the tunnel.

Business Debt:

In the intricate dance of commerce and innovation, businesses often require a partner to help them achieve their dreams of expansion, investment, and growth. That partner often takes the form of debt, a powerful financial tool that can propel businesses to new heights.

Businesses, from small start-ups to global corporations, utilize debt as a means to finance operations, invest in new technologies, expand to new markets, and foster innovation. Debt allows businesses to leverage resources, seize opportunities, and drive economic growth. It is, in many ways, a catalyst for entrepreneurship and progress.

However, excessive corporate debt, when not managed, can result in financial instability, increased vulnerability to economic downturns, and even bankruptcy. The risks of corporate debt are not only shouldered by businesses themselves but extend to employees, shareholders, and the broader economy.

National Debt:

On the grand stage of global economics, governments play a central role in financial affairs, and the magnitude of their actions is often reflected in the scale of their borrowing. The implications of soaring national debts and deficits in many countries are of paramount concern, not just to policymakers but to every citizen.

Governments often turn to debt as a means to fund public initiatives, ranging from infrastructure projects to social programs. National debt is used to bridge budget deficits and to finance public spending. While this approach can offer short-term financial flexibility, it can lead to long-term consequences which are far worse, chaining the entire nation to debt.

As national debts and deficits continue to grow, concerns about financial sustainability and economic stability come to the forefront. High levels of national debt can strain government budgets, as larger portions of public spending are required to service interest payments on the debt. The risk of insolvency and its implications for government services, taxation, and inflation are points of concern for both policymakers and citizens.

As the debt clock continually ticks higher, with the US just passing $33.7 Trillion owed, it underscores a fundamental truth—these debts, in some form, must be repaid. It is the hard-earned income of individuals that ultimately fuels these repayments, in the form of taxes. And although the debt can never actually be repaid, the taxes regardless will continue to rise, perpetuating a never-ending cycle.

To further add fuel to the fire, as the national debt is increased through money printing, so too does inflation, making everything more expensive for the citizens, increasing their cost of living, and thus leaving them with less funds to pay off their own personal debts.

This cycle of mounting debt, rising taxes and increased cost of living, effects not just our quality of life but our entire nations financial stability, economic well-being, and societal equilibrium.

Beyond the financial implications, the debt trap raises ethical questions of a financial system that promotes crippling debt and makes it easily accessible. Is it ethical for financial institutions to profit from individuals' indebtedness? What are the moral dilemmas faced by policymakers who must make choices about national debt and its impact on future generations?

And then in the midst of the complex debt trap, one mustn't overlook the glaring absurdity of owing debts within a system where the very currency used for repayment can be manipulated and printed at will.

When debts become burdensome, governments can opt for what appears to be an easy way out – simply creating more money to meet their obligations. However, in doing so, the citizens suffer, and the hidden chains grow stronger. The cycle repeats, and the level of suffering increases.

The money printed today, becomes tomorrow's chains.

We pause to reflect, while taking a bite of the very remnants of the apple gifted to our child. The simple gift, a fleeting chance for contemplation. A respite in the busy day. We look down at our child, and thoughts drift to our own carefree youth, a stark contrast. We remember how everything seemed easier back then, and how much times have changed. How the cost of living has outpaced income. How personal debt has snowballed into an avalanche. And in those rare moments of utter clarity, we see the frailty of fiat, the mirage of money, and the chains of debt that have been hidden all along.

Chapter 10 -
Fiat Death

"More marks!" I announced enthusiastically, dumping the wheelbarrow out in the middle of the living room.

"That should suffice for now," my little sisters voice weaving a blend of pragmatism with a touch of hope, "This should keep me going for a while."

The once-heavy wheelbarrow clanked as I gently placed it down. My eyes remained fixated on her nimble fingers, magically weaving the currency as if it were delicate fabric. Her resourcefulness was captivating.

"Would you like to give it a try?" sensing my intrigue.

"Me? Um, I'm not...," I hesitated, worried what my friends might think.

"Maybe I should just arrange..." she didn't let me finish my thought, giving me a gentle nudge.

"Come on," she urged, “sit!” I relented and sat down beside her as she continued defiantly tucking, pinning and threading the money; transforming them into a makeshift handbag.

With an amused smile, I couldn't help but voice, "But what will people put in these bags?"

My sister giggled, her laughter providing a momentary splash of vibrance amid the bleak time.

"Maybe you should start with a hat," she suggested, pushing a bunch of marks my way. The idea of crafting a hat from worthless banknotes seemed absurd, yet in this world turned upside down, it felt strangely fitting.

And so, amidst the chaos of economic collapse, we sat together, weaving stories out of paper money, crafting fashion from a sense of desperation, finding valuable pockets of joy and creativity in a world where our currency had lost all meaning.

It's hard to believe in such a world where the very thing you've worked your entire life for, you've painstakingly saved and aspired to get, could be littered in the streets. Discarded as worthless, left to be picked by children with wheelbarrows. The thought, the pain, the ending of the world we know, so immense, we push it far to the back of our minds, we scoff at it, as if it'd never happen to us.

The collapse of Germany's currency during the Weimar Republic created a breeding ground for radical politics and the rise of figures like Adolf Hitler. This period of instability led to catastrophic events, including World War II, the Holocaust, and the use of atomic bombs.

Like the butterfly effect, in which a chain of events can be set in motion; when a dying fiat currency flaps its wings, there is far-reaching consequences. Fiat is not solely to blame for these events, but it acts as a catalyst, often triggering a sequence of destruction — and it's a legacy fiat cannot escape.

Behind every totalitarian rise to power, genocide and mass famine — lurks the shadow of fiat currency. The acts of brutality and devastation exemplify how a currency backed by nothing, and worsened by manipulation, can yield dire outcomes.

So intertwined is death and fiat, that they almost always go hand in hand. Fiat currency is the silent accomplice to death.

It’s the helping bystander to some of history's darkest chapters, perpetuating suffering and destruction in its wake.

The death of a currency, quite literally brings with it, the death of people. Throughout history, an uncomfortable truth repeatedly emerges: fiat currencies are fated to collapse, and with their fall, significant consequences follow.

No fiat currency has ever withstood the test of time. Regardless of the nation, era, or rationale used to justify its creation, all have shared the same fate - devaluation, instability, and eventual worthlessness... “it’s going to ZERO.”

Leaders promise this time will be different, that special circumstances will allow their monetary experiment to buck the trend and succeed, where everything else in the past has failed. And we believe them. We place trust into the currency of the nation where we are born. Because without that faith, the thought is just too hard. It’s this blind trust in inflatable currencies, which goes hand in hand with empire ruin.

In understanding the cyclical nature of empires and their currencies, let's briefly explore historical parallels. Throughout the pages of time, powerful civilizations and empires have risen to incredible heights, only to face inevitable declines. These narratives are not mere footnotes in history but serve as cautionary tales, reflecting the intricate dance between prosperity and downfall.

Consider the following examples:

Roman Empire:
Boom**:** The Pax Romana (Roman Peace) period marked a time of relative stability, economic prosperity, and cultural flourishing. The Romans spearheaded advancements in various fields, from engineering marvels such as aqueducts and intricate road systems to significant strides in the sciences and arts. The great architectural feats of Rome, including the Colosseum and the Pantheon, stand as enduring symbols of their innovative prowess and cultural sophistication.
Death**:** Internal strife, economic decline, military overreach, and political instability, all fuelled by the debasing of its own currency, contributed to the fall of the Roman Empire, which had stood for roughly 1000 years. If one had to have a favourite empire death, this is mine.

Byzantine Empire:
Boom**:** The Byzantine Empire experienced a period of territorial expansion, legal codification, and architectural achievements. The introduction of the Byzantine 'solidus,' a gold coin celebrated for its remarkable purity and consistent weight, symbolized the empire's rock-solid stability. This reliable currency, created using precious gold that we learnt about in chapter 1, played a pivotal role in fostering empire growth.
Death**:** The Byzantine empire faced significant challenges, including external invasions, internal conflicts, and it wasn't just the generals with problems. Like Rome, the economic strain pushed their currency, the once-pure solidus, towards debasement. Changes in the coin's purity, along with the practices of clipping and reducing weight, eroded trust in the currency. The very symbol of their stability had fallen, and so too did their once-thriving empire.

Great Depression (1929-1930s):
Boom: The Roaring Twenties saw economic prosperity and technological advancements, including the widespread adoption of production lines pioneered by visionaries like Henry Ford, the rise of consumer culture, and a booming stock market.
Death: The stock market crash of 1929 triggered the removal of the gold standard, marking the beginning of the Great Depression. This economic downturn led to widespread hardship, soaring unemployment, and significant social upheaval.

Modern Fiat Currencies:
Boom: The post-World War II era witnessed the establishment and a widespread adoption of fiat currencies across the globe, facilitating economic growth and globalization.
Death: Instances of economic recessions, financial crises, and challenges in managing fiat currencies have led to periods of economic downturn and instability. We all feel the effects, whether we identify them or not. Those who identify them the most, have hit the complete bust/death aspect... the likes of Argentina, Greece, and Venezuela serve as stark examples of the vulnerabilities and looming death coming to all fiat systems.

In all these examples, it's the population that's caught off guard. Our human optimism ignores the clear pattern that has emerged over 5000 years of economic history. The unbroken chain of fiat failures links the earliest kingdoms to the global superpowers of today. Fiat failing is part of its very nature. It's a characteristic, a feature, and no empire built on a currency that can be debased, has survived.

To believe that by sheer chance you were born into the exception, with an inflationary currency that somehow will defy the odds, is delusional. Regardless of proclaimed safeguards and regulations, or things being new, modern and different this time... the combination of human nature and unrestrained money printing renders collapse inevitable.

The size, politics or posturing of a country does not make it immune to the economic forces that have toppled far mightier regimes in the past. Vast power or a big army also does not protect against the hard lessons of history. It takes humility to acknowledge that today's financial system walks the exact same path of all that came before.

Accepting fiat's fragility is the first step towards a better future. Understanding that collapse is not a matter of if, but when, is rejuvenating. It's a timing question... on average, failed fiat currencies of the past, held up for about 27 years, before succumbing to their inevitable demise. The circumstances may vary, but the ending remains stubbornly fixed, and a crash is well overdue.

The British pound enjoyed over a century of prominence before devaluation forced it to relinquish the reserve crown. Yet even at its peak, cracks were forming in the once-mighty sterling, hinting its coming fall from grace.

Today, the US dollar has already surpassed the average lifespan, having become a true fiat currency in 1971, 52 years ago. As it passes its 79th year of reserve status, the signs of decline grow increasingly pronounced. Rampant money printing and debts measured in unfathomable trillions are mere symptoms of a deeper sickness.

Faith in the dollar now rests on shaky pillars, unsupported by fundamentals and propped up by blind optimism. As it falls, the crown will pass, just as it shifted from the pound to the dollar in the last century.

When viewed in the context of millennia, todays monetary system amounts to little more than an eccentric experiment with inflationary paper. And like those that have gone before, its days are numbered.

Fiat currencies are temporary, destined to self-destruct. Their collapse, inevitable. But as I talk about the death of empires and currencies, it's equally crucial to consider the erosion of individual control.

Even before a fiat currency collapses, the loss of personal certainty over your own savings becomes glaringly apparent as you entertain the notion, that what you've saved is subject to government policies out of your control. This vulnerability, once acknowledged by individuals, brings with it anxieties about currency devaluation...

Alarming is the realization that what you possess can be created out of thin air. That the money you operate with, and use on a daily basis, may not keep its value. It's this uncertainty that not only affects one's mental state but also hampers their willingness to save, embark on entrepreneurial endeavours, and at its worst, can be the death of our very aspirations and dreams. It's the death of individual control, for when trust in a currency dissipates, so does everything else.

Today's situation stands apart from history in one crucial aspect - the unprecedented scale of global interdependency built upon the dollar. Never before has the entire monetary system, across the world, been tied so tightly to the fate of a single fiat currency. So many nations, businesses and individuals, are all tied to this one currency, in some form or another. This hyper-centralization of finance on the dollar creates systemic risks of colossal size.

As in Rome, the similarities are stacking up, and it's not just the debasing of the currency. The United States, with its extensive network of military bases scattered globally, finds itself thinly stretched. Time and again, the grandest empires in history have faced the most precipitous declines. The simultaneous surge in military spending and the ever-increasing military presence, contribute to a ballooning national debt.

With the house of cards beginning to quiver, central banks hold trillions in hollow US debt, while average citizens face exposure through local currency pegs. The "dollar milkshake theory" describes the inevitable shakeout of every country connected.

The greater the centralization, the steeper the fall. The world has bet unprecedentedly big on one fiat horse. When that horse falters, global finance will be brought down with it.

The governments have two options: admit fault, acknowledge that fiat was a flawed idea, let everything crumble; or, as empires always do, hold on and delay the inevitable. Contagion looms, warnings grow louder, and instability mounts. Yet, the system still lurches forward, unable to break its addiction to printing, even as the foundations are cracking beneath. The death of purchasing power comes to those who don't adapt, a wrecking ball in line with every person, company, and nation.

The drums of war will beat, the violence will be sold as necessary, and the price of everything will continue to rise; with the can being kicked further down the road. Eventually, wheelbarrows will be used to push worthless currency, rendering wars untenable. The illusion of wealth will diminish, and the delayed drawn-out death will be clear as day.

The death of a currency is far more than a death of a currency. An empire is at stake, the people at risk, and looming is our dark history, threatening to repeat.

But it's not the complete end of the world... through collapses, something always grows. Something takes its place, something will rise from the death, blossoming like a flower from the deceased skull of fiat. For better or worse, the cycle begins again. But maybe it doesn't need to be this way. Maybe there is an alternative to the fiat death cycle. Maybe, just maybe... there is a solution.

Bitcoin

After exploring the flaws of our current financial system — the money printing, boom and bust cycles, and ensuing turmoil — your perspective on the dollars in your wallet or numbers in your bank may never be the same.

Hopefully it has answered some questions, and raised some others. For thinking, looking into history, and not blindly accepting the status quo, puts you a step above nearly everyone else.

The revelation, that the money you've worked so hard for, is in fact not money at all, but a currency, backed by nothing, that can be inflated away, and all fiat currencies of the past have shared the exact same fate... it's enough to shake your entire worldview to its core.

It can force you to rethink previously held convictions, look for solutions, and alter your goals entirely. It's as if you've pulled back the veil and realized the landscape of your life, you thought you knew, was entirely different.

Yet the good news is, you have a choice. This pivotal moment is the first step toward grasping the alternative vision laid out in the remainder of this book — a solution aiming to disrupt money itself, and so much more.

So with that, what's the alternative? If not death, then what...

Chapter 11 -
What the F*ck is Bitcoin?

I paced around the living room, arranging an unusual dinner order. "Yes, it's two large pizzas please. One with pepperoni, the other with mushrooms. Oh, and could you cut them into squares, please?"

The pizza shop's operator on the other end seemed a bit bewildered. "Alright, so you're Jercos did you say?"

"Well the order is for a Laszlo," double-checking the Bitcoin Talk page I had opened on my screen. Laszlo had been trying to make this happen for a while, and tonight, we were determined to do something special.

"And the address?" the voice asked, the curiosity building. I started reading the address I had been given, but the man interrupted "W-Wait a minute. Did you say you're paying with what?"

I chuckled. "Yes, Bitcoin. You see, it's a digital currency, and we'd like to use it to pay for the pizzas"

"What's that supposed to mean?" I could feel his patience being tested, with the scepticism in his voice.

"No worries," I said calmly. "I'll just head over in person and pickup, I'll be there in 10"

"Bring cash!" I heard him shout down the line, as I threw the phone on the hook and dashed out.

What you witnessed just now, was the first commercial Bitcoin transaction. The purchase of two pizzas, by Laszlo Hanyecz and facilitated by Jercos (Jeremy Sturdivant). The transaction occurred on May 22, 2010, less than two years after Bitcoin's creation by the pseudonymous entity, Satoshi Nakamoto. Hanyecz paid 10,000 Bitcoin for the two pizzas, which at the time was worth about $41 USD.

This date is now celebrated annually amongst the cryptocurrency community as "Bitcoin Pizza Day." The day Bitcoin met the first principal of money, a medium of exchange.

As we moved forward in this second part of the book, you'll have the opportunity to determine if Bitcoin is money, against the same 6 principals and more than that, you'll be able to consider if it fixes any of the shortcomings, that you uncovered with fiat...

Bitcoin, often referred to as digital gold, is a decentralized digital currency that operates on a peer-to-peer network. This means it's not controlled by any central authority, like governments or banks, and instead, the transactions are recorded on a public ledger called the blockchain.

Since that first pizza purchase, people have used Bitcoin to buy all types of goods and services. But is it money? With our new found understanding of what money is and is not, we can apply the same principles to analyse Bitcoin.

1. Medium of Exchange: Bitcoin enables efficient digital transactions for goods and services, making it a practical and universal currency.

2. Durable: Bitcoin, being a digital currency, doesn't have a physical form like paper money or coins, but it possesses durability in the digital realm. It exists on the blockchain, which is a decentralized and secure ledger, ensuring the integrity and permanence of transactions over time.

3. Divisible: Just like how a dollar can be split into cents, so too can Bitcoin. One Bitcoin is made up of a 100 million smaller units, known as satoshi's. This makes it a practical unit of account for both small and large transactions.

4. Portable: Bitcoin is borderless, people are free to send it, and travel with it, as they wish. As it has no physical form, one could buy Bitcoin in one country, and in essence be dropped into any other country, and as long as they could access a phone or computer, with internet access, they could retrieve their Bitcoins.

5. Scarce: When money cannot be printed away, and the amount is set, the world can stabilize, and the value can hold true. With Bitcoin, there will only ever be 21 million Bitcoins—the supply is fixed, written into its code, and no more can ever exist. As we explored in Chapter 1, gold had maintained its value through scarcity. Similarly, the discovery of Bitcoin through its proof-of-work mining is also gradual and challenging, echoing the enduring principles of scarcity that have historically underpinned the value of precious commodities like gold.

6. Fungibility: Each unit of currency is interchangeable and identical in value. Bitcoin exhibits this principle as each Bitcoin is equal in value to every other Bitcoin. 1 satoshi is 1 satoshi. 1 Bitcoin = 1 Bitcoin. It doesn't matter where a specific Bitcoin comes from; they are all the same and can be used interchangeably in transactions.

As such, whether a country that you happen to be born in, considers it money or not, is irrelevant. The test of money, the 6 principles, is for you to apply, and for you to determine yourself. A country can outlaw it as money, a firm can choose to not accept it, but the principles of what make money, money, remain.

Many attempt to dive headfirst into explaining Bitcoin in isolation, placing their own pre-conceived biases over it. That approach often overlooks the broader context. At its core, Bitcoin is just mathematics, a network of calculations designed to facilitate transactions. Disliking Bitcoin is akin to disliking the number 5 or being upset at the plus sign; it's just maths, a tool, a neutral force.

What it does though, is solve a few very crucial problems. Bitcoin emerged from a pressing need, and its evolution was shaped by years of discoveries and the collective efforts of a small yet vibrant community. This group saw the flaws in fiat, recognized the same issues you've now uncovered, and believed that, just maybe, they could solve it with technology. But to do so, they'd first need to overcome some colossal challenges:

Blockchain Technology: First, the foundational network for Bitcoin was needed. The concept of storing data in blocks and chaining them through cryptographic techniques, gave birth to what we now call the Blockchain. Essentially, it serves as a digital ledger, a recording of all transactions, with no singular database, but instead shared amongst its users.

Mining Incentives: To encourage individuals to participate in the network and secure it, Bitcoin offers mining rewards. Miners receive newly created Bitcoins and transaction fees as rewards for validating transactions. This incentive system was designed to ensure network security.

Scalability: Bitcoin needed to handle an ever-increasing number of transactions as it grew. To address this, Satoshi devised a block size limit and a proof-of-work system that adjusts mining difficulty over time. These measures helped ensure the system could scale while maintaining security.

Security: Bitcoin had to be resistant to various attacks, including Sybil attacks, where an adversary creates multiple fake nodes to manipulate the network, and 51% attacks, where an entity controls the majority of the network's mining power. Through its consensus mechanism, Bitcoin became resilient against these threats.

Privacy: While Bitcoin transactions are visible to all, Satoshi needed to ensure a level of privacy. Transactions are recorded on a public ledger, but the identities of users are concealed behind cryptographic addresses. Maintaining this balance between transparency and privacy was an important design consideration.

Network Governance: Satoshi needed to establish a protocol for network governance, particularly in addressing software updates and changes to the network's rules. The Bitcoin Improvement Proposal (BIP) and the idea of node signalling through mining power are mechanisms for network governance.

Double Spending: The double-spending problem was a significant challenge. It refers to the risk of spending the same bitcoin more than once, which could undermine the integrity of the system. Bitcoin solved this issue by using a distributed ledger (the blockchain) to record all transactions, making it nearly impossible to spend the same Bitcoin twice.

Byzantine Generals' Problem: The Byzantine Generals' Problem relates to achieving consensus in a network of nodes, some of which may be untrustworthy or adversarial. Bitcoin addressed this problem by introducing a proof-of-work mechanism that ensures honest nodes (miners) agree on the validity of transactions and the order in which they are added to the blockchain.

With all those key challenges solved, the stars had aligned, and on the 3rd of January 2009, Bitcoin came to be. Ticking all the 6 properties, mankind for the first time in history, had what could be truly called "perfect money." Something truly scarce, that couldn't be printed away, or more of it discovered.

This was Satoshi's vision, as the mantra goes, "Fix the money, Fix the world," and I believe he's done just that.

But where did Satoshi come from, and is Bitcoin just money?

Unlike the first half of this book, which I suggested reading while perched on the edge of your seat, for this second part of the book, sit back, relax, enjoy a slice of pizza and take comfort. For the death section is over, and there is a rebirth...

Chapter 12 -
Origins and Ownership of Bitcoin

“Off with her f*ckin head!"

The crowd roared with hysteria and the anticipation reached a fever pitch. Until, with a swift and gleaming arc, the shiny guillotine flew down with all its might, and just like that, France had escaped the deathly grip of its intertwined church and state.

Through a tumultuous revolution, they literally separated the two, severed at the neck, heralding a new era of freedom.

America underwent a similar radical transformation, forged through the fires of the Revolutionary War. A leader elected by the people, for the people, marked a departure from the norm, even if the path to get there had been paved in blood.

Now, picture applying the same revolutionary spirit to our money supply. What if there were no single ruler dictating its fate? What if control was shared among the people? A separation of money and state... a currency truly of the people, for the people, by the people.

In the wake of the 2008 financial meltdown, Bitcoin emerged to address problems that had plagued traditional financial systems for centuries, as we explored in the first section of this book.

It was founded on the audacious dream that it could become a genuine currency for the masses, a currency not under the dominion of a solitary authority. Satoshi Nakamoto, the enigmatic creator of Bitcoin, left behind a vision of financial empowerment and freedom, as outlined in his whitepaper, titled "Bitcoin: A Peer-to-Peer Electronic Cash System."

In this document, Satoshi introduced a blueprint for a decentralized form of money, designed to empower individuals and enable direct transactions without the need for intermediaries. This meant that the system would run with no centralized control, no singular database. Instead, the network would be spread across its users. Anyone could join and help run the network, and anyone could interact with the network. It was not tethered to a company, a location, or an entity; instead, it would operate untethered, free, and existing among its users in cyberspace.

The identity of Satoshi remains a well-guarded secret, a deliberate choice to safeguard the fledgling cryptocurrency. His decision to withdraw from the Bitcoin development community exemplified the decentralized essence of the project. Satoshi sought not to become a central authority, a living embodiment of the very problem Bitcoin aimed to solve.

However, Bitcoin's journey was far from solitary. It was imagined, refined, and nurtured by a vibrant community of cypherpunks, early adopters, visionaries, and freedom lovers.

Figures like Adam Back made significant contributions to cryptographic research, including his development of Hashcash, a system that paved the way for Bitcoin's proof-of-work, and Nick Szabo, known for his work on Bit Gold, which predates Bitcoin and provided the intellectual foundations for digital currencies. Following in their footsteps, Hal Finney became the first individual to receive a Bitcoin transaction, sent from Satoshi himself. Wei Dai, a pioneer in cryptography, Gavin Andresen, a leading developer who contributed to Bitcoin's codebase, Martti Malmi and Jeff Garzik, who added their expertise and passion, helped shape Bitcoin into the revolutionary digital currency it is today.

These individuals, alongside countless others, realized the potential of Satoshi's creation. The open-source nature allowed anyone to run Bitcoin's code on their own computer, to contribute and become a part of the network... a co-creator of this decentralized currency.

What started as a concept within a small group of enthusiasts expanded into a global network of thousands of individuals running the code, validating transactions, and securing the Bitcoin blockchain. The decentralized and collaborative nature of Bitcoin's growth stands in stark contrast to what it looks to replace. It's exponential rise, testament to those seeking an alternative.

But one master stroke remained: Satoshi's decision to step away allowed the underlying code to be shared among network operators, with no creator at the helm, in essence, becoming truly decentralized... a currency created by the people, for the people, and of the people.

Unlike the money Satoshi looked to replace, Bitcoin did not bear his face. Just as the French Revolution aimed to separate church from state, Satoshi had separated money from state, and no longer would someone's head bear the currency, it was now free.

With Bitcoin in existence, there was no turning back, no un-inventing it. For it was an idea. The genie was out of the bottle, the people on the path to economic sovereignty and the world would never be the same.

Vive la Bitcoin

Chapter 13 -
Bitcoin's Decentralized Ownership

"Would you like to trade?" the stranger asked, extending his arm towards me.

I looked at him, intrigued by his empty hand, but followed his gaze as he pointed out a colossal stone, a symbol of immense wealth and prestige.

I raised an eyebrow, sceptical yet fascinated, "I wouldn't be able to lift that."

The stranger grinned, "you wouldn't have to," he explained. "I own 1/5th, you give me your goat and I update my notes, saying you now own my part."

I would have raised my eyebrows higher, but they were already maxed out.

Sensing my scepticism, he explained "Mary, she'll write it down too, in her tablet. We all update our ledgers, so we know you own 1/5th of the stone."

Mary nodded in agreement, confirming the stranger's words. I couldn't help but be drawn into this peculiar transaction. It was a daring experiment, "ok, I'm in"

What we just witnessed was a communal ledger, and in a way, decentralized ownership. No set owner of the stone, or the system, or the accounting. It was all shared, communally.

Ledgers like this, whether written or mental notes, shared amongst one another, is one of our oldest forms of money. Pre-dating coins and superior to simple bartering, where one item is swapped for another, this was truly a form of money.

Similarly, Bitcoin operates on the principles of a

decentralized ledger. The blockchain, in the context of Bitcoin, serves as the public ledger that contains a comprehensive record of all Bitcoin transactions. This ledger, however, operates in a digital environment and plays a pivotal role in ensuring the transparency, security, and immutability of Bitcoin.

The blockchain's decentralized nature is a fundamental characteristic that sets Bitcoin apart from traditional financial systems. Unlike conventional ledgers managed by centralized entities, the blockchain is maintained by a global network of nodes. These nodes, operated by individuals and organizations worldwide, collectively validate and record transactions. This decentralized network ensures that no single authority or entity controls the ledger. It's a system of checks and balances, much like the communal ownership of the colossal Rai stones of the Yap islands.

Transparency

One of the blockchain's most remarkable attributes is its unparalleled transparency. Every Bitcoin transaction is recorded on the blockchain and is visible to anyone who cares to inspect it.

This transparency ensures that all transactions are held to the scrutiny of the network, making it highly resistant to fraud and manipulation by any one single entity. Just as with the communal ledger, the blockchain provides a tamper-resistant record that all network participants can access and verify. This transparency builds trust in the system and reinforces the decentralized nature of Bitcoin's ownership.

Inclusivity

One of the most distinctive features of the Bitcoin network is its inclusive nature. Bitcoin is designed to be a financial system open to all, without discrimination or centralized control.

Unlike traditional financial systems, there is no central authority responsible for granting or restricting access to the network. There are no gatekeepers who decide who can or cannot participate.

Democratic

In the world of Bitcoin, every participant has a voice, a role, and the potential to be a part of the decentralized ownership structure, fostering a global community of financial inclusion and self-governance.

People also get to vote! The code is open for anyone to change, and if it's an improvement, others running the code can choose to adopt your version. If enough do, it becomes part of the main Bitcoin code. Likewise, if an update is made by someone and you disagree with it, you have the choice not to run their version. When you actively participate in running the network, your vote matters and is heard.

Miners & Nodes

In the Bitcoin network, two key components play critical roles in maintaining the decentralization: miners and full nodes.

Miners are responsible for solving complex cryptographic puzzles to validate and add new transactions to the blockchain. This process, known as mining, not only secures the network but also ensures the creation of new bitcoins. Miners are distributed worldwide, and the network's security relies on their collective computational power. This global distribution prevents any single entity or group from gaining centralized control.

Full nodes are equally critical, serving as validators of transactions, checking the integrity of every transaction that occurs on the network. Full nodes maintain a complete copy of the blockchain and verify the work of miners. They play a crucial role in enforcing network rules and ensuring the security and consistency of the blockchain.

Choosing to run a node is akin to being a guardian of the Bitcoin network. Individuals who run nodes are directly involved in preserving Bitcoin's decentralization.

They contribute to a collective effort that empowers individuals and upholds the vision of a truly decentralized financial system.

While decentralization lies at the core of Bitcoin's principles, ironically, the community does grapple with centralization and greed, in some ways...

Though Bitcoin aimed to distribute power through trustless systems, centralized exchanges hold custody of user funds, enabling and inviting abuse.

This exposes customers to potential security breaches and theft. If you are in to Bitcoin, you will recognize this flaw... as the mantra goes, “not your keys, not your wallet,” and as such, you would avoid this completely.

Newcomers to the world of Bitcoin, who haven't done their research, may have never heard of the infamous Mt. Gox hack. Instead, they flock to centralized exchanges like FTX, lured by prominent celebrity endorsements, featuring the likes of Matt Damon, Larry David, and Kevin O'Leary in commercials. The shock set in for many, when they discovered that the owner of FTX had been misusing customers' funds.

This type of thing happens all the time, and will continue to do so. Despite crypto's ethos of decentralization, opportunists repeatedly centralize and monetize for personal gain. And while users pile in, for the convenience, truly decentralized networks remove single points of failure by spreading control among users.

Just like with the Rai stones, Bitcoins decentralized ownership, shared and spread amongst the people, is a return to our true roots. Back to how we started, the core of money. And as peoples trust in fiat currencies falters, more will look for alternatives, more will embrace the decentralized nature of Bitcoin and more will say "ok, I'm in.

Chapter 14 -
Preserving Wealth with Bitcoin

"What's this," Mary's eyes darted between the torn handwritten papers, scattered across the board.

"That's um, new money," Alex grinned sheepishly while he continued writing more and more into existence.

"You can't do that," Mary insisted. "The money on the board is what's in play."

"Well, Monopoly instructions say, if the bank runs out, it can print more...'" His voice trailed off, leaving Mary shaking her head in disbelief.

"What a load of..."

Alex cut her off, "Welcome to the real-world sis."

Amid the spirited board game, the addition of this "new money" marked a sudden twist in the dynamics. Little did they know; it would offer a glimpse into the real-world repercussions of tampering with a currency's supply.

As we've witnessed, unchecked power to print endless amounts and banks' ability to loan money they don't even have, has severe consequences. Rampant inflation erodes purchasing power, while cycles of monetary expansion enables corruption.

But is there a way to escape this spiral of devaluation threatening our wealth? Is there a way to "fix" the rules surrounding money, once and for all?

Bitcoin offers a bold new paradigm, not just in its decentralized nature, but also with its fixed money supply. At the heart of Bitcoin lies a supremely important rule - there will only ever be 21 million Bitcoins created. This strict limit is fundamental to Bitcoin's philosophy and cannot be altered. The code itself ensures no more than 21 million

Bitcoins will ever come into circulation.

The concept of scarcity, which has allowed gold to retain its value and shiny allure over the past 5000 years, due to its slow and costly discovery, draws parallels with the way new Bitcoin is created.

Similar to gold, Bitcoin enters circulation gradually through a process known as mining. This digital process involves the creation of a new transaction block on the Bitcoin blockchain, occurring approximately every 10 minutes. Miners play a crucial role in securing the network and are rewarded with newly created Bitcoins as an incentive.

This reward incentive, in fact, halves every 210,000 blocks, roughly every 4 years. This continual halving mechanism ensures the total Bitcoin supply follows a predictable reward schedule, until the maximum of 21 million is eventually reached in the year 2140. At that point, no new Bitcoins will ever be mined again.

It's this predictability that places Bitcoin in a league of its own when it comes to scarcity. Unlike gold, where new discoveries can unpredictably flood the market, Bitcoin's supply increase is 100% known. There are no sudden or unforeseen discoveries; every aspect of its supply is transparent and calculable.

The comparison to fiat currency, with scarcity is of course night and day. Bitcoin's slow inflation rate cannot be manipulated by external policies or corrupt individuals, setting it apart from the unpredictable nature of fiat currency. The mathematical, transparent, and decentralized design stands in stark contrast to the world of endless supply. It shines bright as a beacon of integrity, restoring honesty to the fundamental concept of money.

In fact, Bitcoin is actually deflationary when you take into account amounts being lost. Through accidents and mishaps, it's estimated that the current total supply, as it sits right now, is roughly only 15 million, and that number will only decrease over time.

In a world where inflation poses one of the greatest threats to wealth preservation, Bitcoin is a breath of fresh air. As central banks print money into circulation, existing currency units become less scarce and thus lose purchasing power. What cost $1 today will likely cost $2 or more in the future.

Throughout history, we've seen unchecked inflation decimate savings and rob citizens of hard-earned wealth. The horrors of hyperinflation, where prices can double in days or weeks, have toppled economies and destabilized nations.

Owning scarce assets is a time-tested strategy to hedge against inflation. This is why people universally gravitate towards gold and real estate in times of monetary instability. But unlike gold, which can still be unearthed through heightened mining efforts, and conceivably exists elsewhere in the vast universe, or housing, which can be continuously constructed, and if needed, stretched infinitely towards the sky, Bitcoin's scarcity is unparalleled.

Bitcoin exists as the first truly scarce asset mankind has ever had. With an eternally fixed supply unaffected by geopolitics, it offers refuge to those fleeing the inflationary spiral of fiat currencies. No matter how wildly inflated your local currency supply becomes, one bitcoin will forever remain one bitcoin.

As faith erodes in fiat worldwide, an asset with verifiable scarcity stands poised to provide an escape route to whether the storm. An ark to save citizens from drowning in fiat.

History shows that assets with fixed or scarce supplies reliably preserve wealth and purchasing power over time, while unlimited inflation consistently erodes value.

Reckless money printing has destroyed savings and livelihoods across civilizations. Post-WWI Germany's hyperinflation rendered the marks totally worthless. More recently, Venezuela's unchecked inflation has led to economic collapse.

In countries suffering high inflation like Argentina and Turkey, many now turn to Bitcoin to preserve wealth, as their local currencies depreciate. With Bitcoin, locals can protect their savings against inflation. Even small Bitcoin allocations shield against the rapid inflation eating away at unprotected fiat holdings.

For developed nations, Bitcoin also offers similar protection against the invisible inflation subtly eroding their purchasing power. Even major corporations are now allocating part of their reserves towards Bitcoin, to hedge against currency devaluation, giving them greater confidence in their future and survival.

No matter what, if your country is playing with its own corrupt rule set, bringing new money into life, and washing away your savings, you can opt out. You can walk away from the rigged game. You can choose Bitcoin.

Chapter 15 -
Ending Wars with Bitcoin

"It's happening," my friend burst in. "That's the 14th country to announce... the US will have to follow suit..."

I shrugged, as he continued on, diving head first into his conspiracies." They've probably already started mining, but just haven't publicly admitted it!"

My housemate chimed in, “Well, they could just, um not, right?” but he was quickly interrupted

"No chance, at some point it's a matter of national..."

I cut them all off, remembering something I'd heard long ago on a podcast, "The hash war, it’s here."

This interaction, set in the not-too-distant future, tells of a time Max Keiser predicted, in which wars are fought between nations, using computer mining rather than bullets. Countries would compete for hash power, ushering in a new era of international relations.

We’ve already discussed how the destructive nature of fiat currency leads to war, especially forever wars...

The alternative to this stands Bitcoin. With its fixed supply and decentralized nature, there exists the possibility where its radical nature could bring about a more peaceful world...

Unlike fiat, where wars become a means to sustain the fiat-system, with Bitcoin, war becomes pointless. Bitcoin removes the inflationary motives for nations to conduct military operations and wars.

Where fiat currency leaves a trail of destruction; Bitcoin paves a path to a brighter future.

A world in which countries engage in a battle for supremacy, not with tanks and soldiers, but with computational power.

The concept of nations competing for hash power on the Bitcoin network would redefine geopolitical strategy. The underlying principle is simple yet profound: countries embracing Bitcoin gain a distinct advantage over those who resist.

Bitcoin's decentralized nature means that the nation with the most significant share of the network's hash power holds a powerful position. As the benefit of embracing this new form of power becomes evident, the rush to secure mining supremacy ensues.

Real-world examples of nations, like El Salvador, adopting Bitcoin are inspiring tales of diplomatic innovation, in which other countries will follow. El Salvador is moving to secure hash power, through making use of their biggest renewable resource — volcanos.

Rather than resorting to armed conflicts and traditional warfare, countries have found a non-violent channel to assert their influence. Nations worldwide will invest in Bitcoin mining, aligning their interests with securing the network and vying for a stronger position in the global arena.

The Bitcoin revolution extends beyond digital currency; it is a transformation of international relations and diplomacy. The decentralized, transparent, and immutable nature of the blockchain will reinvent the way countries interact on the global stage. Trust is no longer a matter of negotiations and treaties, but is mathematically guaranteed. Bitcoin's impact on diplomatic dialogue, dispute resolution, and international cooperation is nothing short of revolutionary.

With Bitcoin at the heart of international finance, nations have more to gain by maintaining peaceful relations, than resorting to military force. The risk of economic isolation and potential backlash from the global Bitcoin community discourages aggression. A world where Bitcoin's principles guide global power dynamics is a world where the destructive motivations for war become obsolete.

The potential benefits of a world where Bitcoin disrupts the destructive fiat cycles are immeasurable. With the reduction of traditional war incentives, nations could allocate resources to innovation and prosperity instead of conflict. With economies anchored in sound money, nations can focus on shared interests and collaborations, laying the foundation for a more prosperous and peaceful world.

In the face of this new reality, individuals and nations must make a choice. They can perpetuate the path they are on, a path of "forever wars," fuelled by fiat, or embrace the road to hash wars instead, through Bitcoin. Forever wars or Forever peace. Bitcoin or death in its purest form.

Bitcoin is peace.

Chapter 16 -
Bitcoin is saving the planet

The air was charged with anticipation as dignitaries from a once energy-starved nation gathered for the grand unveiling of their first Bitcoin-powered nuclear power plant.

"So let me get this straight," one reporter inquired, leaning in with scepticism, "we're going to use nuclear to mine Bitcoins?"

"Yes, but no," the host replied with a smile, adding to the intrigue. "Bitcoin has made this plant possible. Their miners are going to be our first buyer of power..."

I turned to my friend next to me and whispered, "How's this help us?"

"Well, how's your energy bill looking?" he replied. My gut sank at the mere thought.

He continued, "You enjoy the blackouts? The dirty coal? The damage to the planet..."

"Ok, Ok," I conceded, joining in the clapping as the ribbon was cut.

In a time when the world grapples with energy challenges and nations scramble for solutions, the situation appears precarious. Hefty investments are made, base power is aggressively cut and nations are pinning their hopes on technological advancements to save the day.

But amid the uncertainty, there's a glimmer of hope. Green energy solutions are emerging, and Bitcoin is playing a pivotal role in making them viable. Whether it's opening the doors to nuclear energy, capturing and reducing harmful gases associated with flaring and landfills, or unlocking the power of volcanoes; Bitcoin is at the forefront of charting new, eco-friendly paths to sustainable energy sources.

As we've discussed previously, the ecological effects of fiat-based currencies is immense, with the potential to harm our planet irreparably. However, Bitcoin offers an alternative, a more sustainable future, a cleaner and greener environment for all.

Energy created in one location, like El Salvador, utilizing electricity generated from a volcano's geothermal energy, can be used to mine Bitcoin. This Bitcoin can then be transmitted across the world, where a person in a remote area can use the Bitcoin to pay their local energy supplier to power their own lights. It's now not merely a matter of sending digital bits or currency; it's about transmitting power.

Bitcoin is a store of power. The power you use in mining, which rewards you in Bitcoin, can then be transferred anywhere on the planet, and used to redeem power there.

This is a decentralization of our energy grids, across borders, and opens up brand new paths of innovation and abilities to lower costs of green energy.

In regards to nuclear, often the initial upfront financial burden, becomes the limiting factor, making it out of reach for many nations. When a new plant opens up, getting enough customers, from day one, becomes a major issue, as if it doesn't, the debt it holds becomes too much of a burden.

With the addition of Bitcoin miners, seeking affordable and sustainable energy sources, it means a nuclear plant can open, with a guaranteed buyer of any excess additional power not being used by its customers. This provides a reliable source of revenue, helping cover debt repayments and making the establishment of nuclear plants more financially viable.

And then because of that guaranteed first buyer, these plants become financially feasible, in countries which could have never dreamed of affording them before. Countries which, because of their poverty, usually are reliant on the dirtier power solutions as their only options.

Time and time again, Bitcoin is finding renewable energies, as it naturally seeks out cheap power. A lot of this power, which exists on the planet, readily available, goes uncaptured because a purchaser in need of the power is not nearby. E.g. There is no city close enough to make it profitable.

Bitcoin's unique capability to act as a reliable buyer of such uncaptured energy not only makes it financially viable but also demonstrates its potential to drive innovation in the energy sector. This interconnectedness between Bitcoin and energy production is a unique aspect, underscoring Bitcoin's capacity to incentivize energy efficiency and promote sustainability.

Another area Bitcoin is already helping the planet, is with waste management. Typically, when waste is disposed of in landfills, it must remain there for many years as the land slowly degrades the waste, and the land becomes usable once more.

During this process, landfills emit harmful methane gas. Methane gas, which would otherwise be released into the atmosphere, is now being captured at landfills. Bitcoin mining operations, seeking cost-effective energy sources, set up small facilities to capture and utilize this methane for

Bitcoin mining, instead of it going into the atmosphere.

The reason this gas wasn't being captured, is because it produces a low and unreliable power output, making it unprofitable. However, Bitcoin has changed the landscape by turning this gas into a profitable energy source. These initiatives are already underway, as Bitcoin miners partner with landfills to make our waste management more environmentally friendly.

Additionally, Bitcoin's positive impact extends to addressing the problem of gas flaring at oil and gas facilities. Gas flaring is a practice where excess natural gas, often released during oil extraction, is burned off into the atmosphere. It's a wasteful and environmentally harmful process. However, some forward-thinking Bitcoin mining operations have found a solution in capturing and utilizing this previously wasted resource. By setting up small facilities to capture and convert the emitted gas into electricity for Bitcoin mining, Bitcoin contributes to the reduction of harmful emissions and makes waste management more environmentally friendly. These initiatives demonstrate how Bitcoin's profit-driven approach can lead to innovative solutions that align with economic benefits and a greener environment.

Innovation often thrives when profit is the driving force. When nations awkwardly rush to force green initiatives without economic incentives, they risk shifting the environmental burden to other countries. Leading by example is admirable, but in the real world, it can be impractical and even worst on our planet.

Real change happens when cost savings and profitability is helping advance the energy sector. When 'doing the right thing' aligns with economic benefits, companies and nations eagerly embrace change, not for virtue signalling but for the tangible advantages it brings to their own economies and progress.

The fallacy that, Bitcoin is intrinsically bad because it uses power, is so absurd, it deserves to be ridiculed. This misconception is often perpetuated by politicians who seek to exert control over their citizens.

Using power, especially truly renewable forms that don't destroy the planet, should be our goal.

Instead of restricting energy use, we should aim to capture and use MORE power. Human progress is intertwined with our ability to harness and utilize energy. It's counterproductive to manipulate and frighten citizens into shrinking their footprint to the extent that it stifles progress and hinders their ability to fully live, especially why those encouraging it are jet setting all over the globe constantly.

Bitcoin stands against that, and Bitcoin is a potential gateway to something much more...

Eventually, if we want to become a 'Type 2 civilization', as proposed by Michio Kaku, or even a Type 1, we need to consume power. And we need to get good at it. This is our path to the stars. The ability to harness power. Bitcoin enables it. Bitcoin is our gateway to the galaxy, our road to a brighter future...

In a world facing energy challenges and environmental concerns, Bitcoin offers a ray of hope. From unlocking the potential of renewable energy sources to revolutionizing waste management and sustainable finance, Bitcoin is paving the way towards a greener future. The choice is clear – continue down the fiat road of ecological devastation or embrace a new path that promotes responsible finance, environmental stewardship, and, perhaps one day, a journey to the stars.

Chapter 17 -
Bitcoin for Global Impact

Engrossed in my textbooks, deep within the library, I crammed as much for my final exam that my rattled brain would allow. Out of the corner of my eye, a guy who had taken a seat nearby, offered a friendly smile.

I smiled back and took a sip of my coffee. If only he knew the immense stress I was under.

He sat at his laptop, probably researching holiday destinations, a stark contrast to my academic turmoil.

And that's when I saw them – two men dressed in dark suits approaching, their presence growing more menacing with each step. They stopped right beside the man who had smiled. It was in that moment I knew the encounter was anything but ordinary.

Leaning in with all my inner might, whilst trying to look relaxed, I heard the word "FBI" as the other signalled that he wanted the laptop to remain open. And before I knew it, more people had walked in, and quickly the man was stood up, and whisked away. The library that was once a sanctuary of study had transformed into an unexpected scene of intrigue.

It would be disingenuous to skimp over the fact that Bitcoin has been used, as means of payment, for illegal goods. Especially in its infancy.

What we just witnessed, in the library dramatization, was Ross William Ulbricht get arrested, for running a decentralized marketplace known as the "Silk Road."
On this marketplace, it was up to the user to obey their own local laws. Like the town square, if a crime takes place within it, the police don't go and arrest the Mayor of the town, just because the crime took place on his land and on his watch. That was the theory the owners of the site had anyway.

The marketplace, though, was inadvertently used for all

types of criminal purchases, and as such, the law didn't see the owners as guilt free, and ultimately the creator, to this day, is still in jail.

Whether he was in the right or wrong, that was a matter for the courts. What shouldn't be lumped in with the guilt, is the means of payment. These days, the majority of Bitcoin transactions are not crime related at all, but yes, like many new technologies, Bitcoin first got its more mainstream use in darker corners.

Far from the days of the Silk Road, Bitcoin has grown into something much more significant than its early associations with the dark web. It has transcended the stigma of crime to become a transformative force, having huge positive impacts around the globe.

Let's explore these impacts in more detail...

Financial Inclusion:
Bitcoin's decentralized nature and borderless accessibility make it a powerful tool for financial inclusion. It serves as a lifeline for those who are unbanked or underbanked, providing access to financial services that were previously out of reach for millions.

As of March 2023, approximately 1.7 billion adults, or roughly 24% of the global adult population, were unbanked, underscoring the pressing need for solutions like Bitcoin to bridge this financial gap and extend banking access to everyone.

Remittances:
Bitcoin has become an essential tool for secure cross-border remittances. It offers an efficient and cost-effective means for people to send money to their loved ones across the world. In regions suffering from financial instability, Bitcoin has been a lifeline for those affected by economic crises and political turmoil.

Humanitarian Efforts:
Bitcoin offers a transparent and efficient way to deliver aid, track donations, and provide relief in crisis-stricken areas. Its decentralized and trustless nature ensures that aid reaches those who need it most, without the inefficiencies associated with traditional aid distribution, where a significant portion of funds can get eaten up in administration fees and salaries.

Environment:
As explored in the previous chapter, Bitcoin is actively spurring innovation in the renewable energy sector and transforming waste management practices. This isn't mere conjecture but a concrete reality. As an increasing number of individuals, businesses, and countries embrace Bitcoin, the favourable environmental outcomes will grow, concurrently diminishing the adverse consequences associated with fiat currencies.

Multi-Planetary:
Progress requires momentum. If you're not growing, you are dying. If your technology is not moving forwards, you are going backwards. We see this detailed no better than in our space efforts.

In the 1960s, the frenzied race to the moon spawned

relentless technological advancements, culminating in humanity's first steps on the Moon. But after this monumental achievement, stagnation set in. The costs of maintaining shuttle programs was deemed excessive, missions dwindled, and we retreated from the cosmos.

Decades passed with no return to the Moon. The spark that ignited our extra-terrestrial ambitions faded. NASA's funding declined steadily, and without a bold national vision, space lost its priority.

But this story need not be our destiny. Nor should we be chained to this planet forever. Bitcoin sets the stage for a new Space Age, not driven by the geopolitical arena, but by global collaboration. With individuals unified in driving human progress.

The path upward beckons. By taking steps grounded in principles of transparency, decentralization, and empowerment, we tread a trail blazed by Bitcoin. This mindset alone can propel us to new heights. With the added advantage of being liberated from the constraints of cyclical boom and bust patterns, our progress can seamlessly compound upon itself... to the moon & beyond, we will live amongst the stars.

Couple all these with the theory of reduced wars, reduced debt, reduced pain and suffering, it becomes more than just the transformation of money; and instead about the preservation of a dream. An endeavour to redefine the broken world we live in.

In the face of fiat-based inequality and instability, Bitcoin, once portrayed as just a currency for criminals, now represents the potential for an equitable, secure, and inclusive financial system.

It offers a vision of a future where financial control is decentralized, destructive fiat cycles are disrupted, individuals have control over their destinies and humanity can resume our path of progression into the stars. Bitcoin stands as the hope, opportunity and life.

Chapter 18 -
Religion and Bitcoin

In the heart of the cryptocurrency world, there's an awe-inspiring tale of faith and audacity that never fails to stir the soul.

Picture this: the year was 2016, and Bitcoin, the digital marvel, was just a fledgling asset trading at a humble $900. Didi Taihuttu, a Dutch national, shared an extraordinary vision with his wife and three daughters – to sell everything they owned and place their faith in Bitcoin.

As they made the decision to let go of their house, cars, motorbikes, holiday home, and every earthly possession, a sense of exhilaration coursed through their veins. Their inspiration? A belief that went beyond conventional understanding. They saw Bitcoin not just as a digital currency but as immutable and incorruptible code. That no matter what happened in the world, there would only ever be 21 million — a rule etched so deep into the heart of Bitcoin, it was akin to an unbreakable commandment.

The Taihuttu family's journey was an adventure driven by an unwavering belief in something that remained resolutely unchangeable in a world of constant flux. It was not a faith in a divine entity but in a new currency that had the power to change lives. This belief was so strong that it led them to embrace a future unburdened by material possessions.

Bitcoin's trustless and decentralized design resonates with those seeking a moral anchor, in today's ethically questionable world. Interestingly, as Didi knew, Bitcoin operates under its own set of morals and principals, akin to a set of commandments. These are etched into its very code, unchangeable and unwavering. Just as the moral "thou shalt not steal" is a religious ideal, written into the collective conscience, Bitcoin adheres to a parallel doctrine — one of unalterable rules and protocols. As such, to some, Bitcoin evokes a religious devotion. It attracts an almost cult-like following, yet its draw stems from more than just fanaticism.

The driving force that's guiding people away from fiat currency, is ultimately leading them to Bitcoin. The discovery and feeling of being able to trust in a steadfast certainty is like a revelation.

For many, their bitcoin experience is so unique, it's something they may have never encountered before – a glimpse into a world where the rules are set in stone and followed to the letter, regardless of authority. It's this sensation, and the unwavering integrity and belief in the system, that has people worshipping, at least financially, at the altar of Bitcoin.

Similarly, in alignment with this trend, El Salvador has risen as the temple. With the small Central American country embracing Bitcoin as legal tender and President Nayib Bukele leading the way, expats have been flocking to destinations like El Zonte, also referred to as Bitcoin Beach. As if on a rite of passage, they revere it as a sanctuary of freedom, a haven they deeply admire — something they wish their own fiat-driven countries would embrace.
At the same time, the inverse is also happening. Followers of religions around the world, are finding meaning and faith in the technical enlightenment of Bitcoin's cryptographic security and mathematical truths.

The unifying and common aspect being the unchangeable, uncompromising code that both adhere to. There crisscrossing interplay, as both strive to provide fixed moral frameworks, liberation, and shaping the world for the better.

While faith in our systems of government, rule and trust crumble, Bitcoin's unwavering code is something we can all have faith in, and its philosophy is one that unites its users on a global scale.

For every person who has lost trust in the old financial structures and rediscovered it again in the promise of Bitcoin, there is one who comes to Bitcoin already cultivated in enduring values by their spiritual traditions. And there's even Bitcoiners, discovering religions for the very first time...

Either way, Bitcoin beckons those searching for meaning in an unpredictable world. Whether etched into the digital currency or passed down through generations of faith, unwavering code connects people at the deepest level. Tapping into humanity's innate yearning for truths and beliefs.

Chapter 19 -
Bitcoin's Promise

Imagine a child born into this world, eyes curious and eager to learn. His parents, Maria and Rafael, wanted for their child, the best opportunities possible; unlike they had grown up with.

Maria and Rafael live in a tiny remote village where only a few hundred people reside. Yet, they are part of the 1.7 billion individuals who find themselves unbanked, living in an area of the world where no traditional bank will open.

For years, they struggled to find a safe place to store their hard-earned money and access basic financial services. Without access to a bank, they resorted to informal lending methods with exorbitant interest rates, setting themselves up for a cycle of debt that seemed impossible to break free from.

But the world was changing, and Bitcoin had reached even the most remote corners of the globe. With a simple smartphone and access to the internet, Maria and Rafael discovered a financial lifeline. Bitcoin had become their gateway to financial inclusion, in a world that had not barred them, but never even acknowledged their existence.

This newfound financial access empowered them to send and receive money, make investments, and save for the future. For years, they had wanted, demanded, and wished for a bank, only to realize they no longer needed one. They could be their own bank, and in a way, rendered obsolete the very banks that had excluded them.

With their own digital wallets, they held the keys to their financial destinies, unlocking access to a better world.

Their child, born a Bitcoin baby, marked the dawn of a new era in financial empowerment and self-sovereignty, that was unimaginable just a generation ago. Their child would grow up in a world where financial limitations were a thing of the past, and where everyone, no matter where they were born, had the opportunity to be financially free.

In chapter 9, we delved deep into how fiat-based systems drive the accumulation of debt. In this chapter, we shift our focus to the potential liberation from this trap, and the promise of Bitcoin.

Bitcoin offers an escape route that can transform individuals and communities. It represents a paradigm shift—a move from the familiar debt-ridden world, to a realm of financial empowerment and independence. While fiat is debt, bitcoin is financial empowerment.

Let's embark on a journey into Bitcoin's promise of financial empowerment:

Financial Inclusion

As touched on, one of the most potent ways Bitcoin offers an escape from the debt trap is through financial inclusion. This digital currency extends a helping hand to the unbanked and underbanked populations, those who often find themselves excluded from the traditional financial system, pushed further into the shadows of debt.

Many individuals in the world, roughly 24%, do not have access to basic financial services. They are deprived of the ability to open bank accounts, apply for loans, or even have a safe place to store their hard-earned money.

This is because operating a bank, in their area, would not be profitable, and banks are driven by profit. In the absence of these financial tools, they often resort to informal lending methods with exorbitant interest rates, setting themselves up for a cycle of debt that can be incredibly challenging to break free from.

Bitcoin steps in, providing a decentralized, borderless, and accessible way for anyone with an internet connection to participate in the global economy. With a smartphone or computer, individuals in remote or underserved regions can now access a digital wallet, send and receive money, make investments, and save for the future.

What makes this so satisfying is that, unlike those living fully immersed in the fiat system, this is not asking someone to leave a bank. Instead, the banking system truly does not give a shit about them, and never has. As such, they are getting access to a new financial service, without needing any convincing of replacing an old one.

Moreover, Bitcoin's design eliminates the need for intermediaries, reducing transaction costs, which can be another barrier to financial services. By enabling direct peer-to-peer transactions, it allows individuals to take control of their own financial destinies without being subjected to the whims of banks and exorbitant fees.

By promoting financial inclusion, Bitcoin becomes a powerful tool in preventing individuals from falling into the cycle of debt. It equips them with the means to handle their finances, invest wisely, and build financial security.

Self-Sovereignty

The inclusion and ability to manage one's own finances, represents a level of self-sovereignty rarely seen in the world of finance.

In the conventional financial system, individuals must trust financial intermediaries: banks, payment processors, and other institutions — to manage their finances. This trust often comes with conditions and obligations that can lead to debt, whether it's in the form of account fees, loan interest, or the loss of control over their assets. In essence, the traditional system leaves individuals at the mercy of financial gatekeepers, a precarious position that can lead to the debt trap.

Bitcoin upends this status quo by giving users full control over their financial assets. With Bitcoin, individuals are their own banks. We call it BYOB... Be Your Own Bank. They hold the keys to their digital wallets and no entity can interfere with their transactions or seize their funds without consent.

This profound shift from relying on intermediaries to becoming one's financial custodian, is the ultimate in financial responsibility. Users are accountable for the safety and management of their own digital assets.

Of course, with the responsibility of Self-Sovereignty, comes its pitfalls. However, this is a feature, not an issue. Nearly everyone in "crypto" has experienced something like this, some loss of funds. This stands testament to the control you personally have over it. It's yours to hold, and yours to lose.

Whether it be from placing your trust in someone you shouldn't have, sending to a wrong address, or using an exchange that gets hacked, this is not an issue with Bitcoin, but with your own decisions.

The Bitcoin protocol itself has never been hacked. Ultimately, your interaction and experience with Bitcoin is your responsibility. There is no one to complain to, no minister to protect you, no law to bail you out and no CEO to protest against. The user control and sovereignty that

Bitcoin promotes, is a philosophical underpinning of financial self-determination. You are in charge and that's freedom.

"Getting" Bitcoin

One of Bitcoins greatest gifts, when it comes to financial empowerment, is teaching everyone "what money is." When people interact with it, receive it, or delve into its intricacies, it sparks a continuous cycle of questions and discovery. Bitcoin serves as a powerful tool to demystify the nature of money, inviting all who engage with it to explore not just Bitcoin's fundamental principles, but the fiat-currency it opposes.

Once someone truly "gets it", the dual meaning, is poetic. It has been said, we "get bitcoin" at the price we deserve. That is, understanding Bitcoin, what it is and what it solves... once you "get" what it is... that's when you "get it", as in, you accumulate some.

Doing so usually requires a number of hurdles. Which many people, to this day, have not gotten over. They are:

- Being able to analyse something on its own merits, without your own biases effecting your views. Without the world in which you were born into, effecting your views. Without your friends, family and media effecting your views.

- Not being discouraged about the "price" of Bitcoin, determined in your local fake currency. For if that is an issue, and you'd rather hold the fiat, you haven't understood it at all.

- Once you get some, not having sold as soon as it ticks up or down slightly in price, leaving you back out, with the worthless notes.

- Not getting greedy, delving into shit coins, and getting rekt on them to the point you bail out.

- You have to survive the knocks: the initial mistakes like trusting an exchange that gets hacked, sending to the wrong address or falling for a guy shouting “Biiiiiiiiiiiiitconnnnnnneeeeeeeecct” on a stage.

Once you can get pass all that, take the hits, and for many it does take multiple, but once you understand it, that is when you get it. The price you are in at, is the price you deserve. For Bitcoin is the ultimate IQ test, mixed with endurance.

Privacy and Freedom

Privacy and freedom are also central to Bitcoin's ethical framework. Its creator, a master of privacy, mirrored this ethos in the network. Bitcoin empowers individuals to transact and store wealth privately, free from intrusive surveillance. Preserving financial privacy is an ethical imperative, respecting individuals' rights to manage their finances without unwarranted scrutiny.

On the other end of the spectrum, governments salivate over the potential control offered by a 'Central Bank Digital Currency' (CBDC). These are the same entities that, with their fiat currencies, are responsible for financial turmoil. They take the concept of digital currencies, remove the very qualities that make them so liberating, and layer them to the hilt with extensive restrictions.

Societal Impact

The societal impact of Bitcoin's financial empowerment, especially in relation to avoiding the debt trap, is profound. When individuals can manage their own finances, without falling into a cycle of debt, it reverberates throughout society.

Unburdened by debt-related obligations, people have the financial capacity to invest in productive ventures and opportunities. This, in turn, fuels economic growth and job creation. Reduced income inequality follows as a consequence, as more people have the means to lift themselves from financial hardship. Furthermore, this extends into spheres such as innovation, as people have the financial freedom to support creative endeavours and entrepreneurial ventures.

In a real-life example, on both an individual and state level, Bitcoin is empowering the unbanked people of El Salvador. Through the official adoption of Bitcoin as their second recognized currency, the nation has provided its citizens with access to a truly inflation-resistant means of saving, thus expanding their liberties and witnessing newfound economic growth.

While the promise of Bitcoin's financial empowerment is evident, it's not without its challenges and concerns. Regulatory issues, in particular, pose a significant hurdle.

Nevertheless, in the grand tapestry of financial evolution, individual sovereignty remains the cornerstone, and the allure of Bitcoin as the hardest money holds a timeless promise, already reshaping the financial landscape and our world.

By empowering individuals and communities to have greater control over their own finances, it provides a vision of a decentralized future, where financial freedom is not the exception but the norm. Where everyone born into it, is born free.

Chapter 20 -
Life

"3000 years, and we're still standing," Senator Vita whispered, his eyes fixed on the tablet, the genesis block. The engraved symbols were cryptic, yet the power they held was undeniable.

As the other senators gathered around, tales of the past filled the chamber - hushed voices speaking of days when Rome stood on the brink, when ceaseless battles soaked the land in blood, when stability was but a fleeting dream.

Vita ran his fingers over the tablet—a relic from an age of upheaval, now the bedrock upholding the interstellar civilization.

"Here stands, what has always been, our key to the universe," Vita proclaimed, while the first reports of their thriving new colony in Alpha Centauri flashed up on hovering screens behind him.

"In the grand tapestry of the heavens, it is fitting that we find our reach expanding in the Centaurus constellation, named after the wise and healing god, Chiron. Much like Chiron, we too have evolved and healed from our past. Today marks our fifth colony amongst the stars, with many more to come, for our trajectory is unwavering and true."

Senators from across the empire nodded and erupted in applause, their presence not limited to the physical realm alone. Holographic counterparts seamlessly mingled, with just as much enthusiasm and engagement as those attending in person.

That afternoon, they participated in governance through decentralized autonomous organizations, and engaged in transparent, tamper-proof elections by casting their votes on the blockchain.

The decentralized nature of Bitcoin had severed the cycles of violence and collapse, ushering in a state of constant harmony. With Bitcoin as its backbone, Rome had expanded far beyond its ancient borders, the scope of its civilization truly interstellar.

Despite their progress, all roads still converged into this one location, the heart of Rome, just as all threads of their progress ultimately wove back to Bitcoin, the singular foundation upholding their forever-empire.

Stepping out of the senate chamber, Vita walked beneath towering marble pillars, encased in laser fields. The vast halls held the wisdom of generations, preserved throughout the ages, and existing for everyone, through their decentralized internet.

Outside, he breathed in the fresh and pure air, undisturbed by the sleek spacecraft gliding pass ancient monuments. As daylight waned, supply ships illuminated the sky, seamlessly transitioning into light speed. Bound for celestial outposts; blockchain technology guaranteed secure commerce, across space and time.

Citizens browsed market stalls, purchasing goods with cryptographic keys. The Roman people had embraced blockchain into every aspect of their daily life. Cryptographic fluency as essential as Latin itself.

In the background, the pristine Colosseum stood as a symbol of both ancient glory and technological prowess, now hosting virtual gladiator battles in augmented reality. This synergy was Rome's genius - applying modern innovations upon the bedrock of time-tested values. The same vision that built their empire across continents, now spanned entire solar systems.

Rome had harnessed the power of Bitcoin, the currency of life, to build a civilization of unparalleled freedoms. Rome was forever, created with the same vision and vigour of the ancient civilization, its modern rebirth existing amongst the stars.

An alternative timeline, in which the Roman Empire survived, is a tantalizing concept indeed. As I said, at the start of this book, to understand the advantages of Bitcoin, we truly had to dive into history. Only by immersing ourselves in tales of the past, can we now fathom a Rome in 3000AD, and more importantly, forge our own unique path.

This chapter is about life. A return to our roots. Older than money itself, was the ledger we discussed. A way of accounting and that's all Bitcoin is, a public ledger. Backed by maths and the laws of the universe.

If gold is Gods money, Bitcoin is humanities money. Woven into our DNA; created by us, for us, always a part of us and always there to be discovered by us.

As the mantra goes, "Fix the money, Fix the world," and thrust are we, into Satoshi's vision, guardians of his creation and beneficiaries of his dream. The currency of life.

As I refer to Bitcoin as life, and fiat as death, a peculiar irony emerges - a recurring proclamation of Bitcoins demise. But like the Terminator which just won't die, Bitcoin has been declared "dead" a staggering 474 times at the time of this writing. It's an ironic dance, a perpetual cycle of obituaries, as journalists, eagerly line up, blowing their trumpets to declare the technology lifeless. They parade up and down, forecasting the demise of Bitcoin, only to witness its continued survival, over and over.

The common thread in these premature eulogies always revolves around their own beliefs, the price action of it in their local shit-coin fiat currency, and without ever addressing any scrutiny upon their own monetary system.

The amusement lies not only in the frequency of these articles, akin to walking over a rake and constantly getting slapped, but also in the underlying motivation behind them. As Bitcoin survives and thrives, you can taste the salt in the air of every journalist that has declared it dead, and has to live with it rising like a phoenix, as the exact opposite of what they predicted comes true. It lives, and there's nothing they can do about it.

Will governments attempt to squash this dream? Absolutely. Will they try switching their citizens to a CBDC? Sure. But countries don't exist in a vacuum. Others, especially those which have felt the brunt of a fiat-backed system, will choose Bitcoin. As these nations break away, so too will the grip of the remaining countries weaken.

In the end, as it always has been, the hardest money wins. The news media will shout one thing, so called experts will shout another. Let them shout. Let them cry. For we have history, we choose Bitcoin, we choose life.

The orange pill isn't an alternative monetary system, it's the f*ckin anecdote to a dying one. It's the medicine to survive our collapsing system.

For once our faith in false money loses its shine, people can begin to build back on sound foundations.

By now, you've learnt, fiat currency isn't merely a financial system, nor is it just currency in our pocket, but instead it's a death sentence in disguise. Bitcoin, in contrast, offers a lifeline to escape the blood-soaked fiat.

Through its wars, disparities and erosion of wealth, the death is no longer hyperbole, but reality. It's here, knocking at the door. Where fiat thrives on death, Bitcoin thrives on life.

And although changing monetary systems can be turbulent times, crisis do offer opportunity. More millionaires were made during the great depression, than any other period in history. With Henry Ford bringing out the Model T in 1908 during the stock market panic and the 2008 GFC giving rise to Tesla and Bitcoin, time and again, crises offer not just doom, but opportunity.

As fiat crumbles and death creeps in all around, Bitcoin stands as humanity's hope. Fiat's funeral march is the backdrop to Bitcoin's rise as the currency of life. A new beginning. A potential end to the cycle of destruction. Our forever Rome.

The natural cycle, lived by us, details the ebbs and flows, the booms and busts. But what if it didn't have to be that way. What if each great empire didn't have to fall. What if an empire was untouchable by humanities own shortcomings.

Rome fell, because it did not have Bitcoin.

But the empire of Bitcoin, lives amongst us all, and eventually all roads will lead to it.

Imagine our empire, reaching its peak with sciences, technology, and medicines all dedicated to bettering ourselves. And then, as the cycle reaches its end, instead of crumbling, sending everything back into the dark ages, and our currency joining the skulls of the fallen, instead, it just kept blossoming.

We'd live longer, we'd be happier, we'd conquer the stars and we'd be immortal.

I hope you found this journey enlightening and thought-provoking. As you close this book, remember the question which once may have sounded dramatic, but now, with the knowledge you've gained, holds a profound significance. What you choose, Bitcoin or Death, matters, not just for you, but for the future of humanity.

The question is answered through the actions you take. While your views and expressions on the topic may differ, your ownership of Bitcoin or fiat serves as the ultimate answer.

Share the question, explore its depths, and let it guide you on a path to understanding and, perhaps, to a brighter future. This question is yours to carry, a torch of enlightenment in a world fraught with uncertainty: Bitcoin or Death?

Sharing the Question?

Thanks for reading this book, and for even considering the question 'Bitcoin or Death?' ...that's all that was required.

Decentralized money, nodes, hash rates—the jargon gets overwhelming, our family glazes over, our friends tune out, but the question was all we needed.

It's a question I hope you can share with your loved ones. It is clear and concise, laying forth only two options: accepting the current system and the historical implications of fiat currencies, or taking a different route. The ultimate orange pill, a mere question, with only 2 options. It gets people thinking, and allows them to come to their own conclusions.

Please share the question with your friends,
family & relatives at:

BitcoinOrDeath.com

Bitcoin or Death Challenge

Congratulations on navigating the thought-provoking pages of "Bitcoin or Death." Now, as you emerge from the depths of its insights, a new journey awaits—a 3-part challenge designed to immerse you in the profound choice between embracing Bitcoin's transformative potential or adhering to the confines of the existing system.

In a world where decisions shape destinies, your choice between Bitcoin and the status quo isn't just a financial decision—it's a philosophical stance. This challenge encourages you to not merely adopt Bitcoin but to actively engage with the transformative power it offers.

As you embark on this challenge, it begins with a symbolic act—an act of commitment etched into the very pages of the book. Choose your stand boldly by marking your decision within the book itself. This tangible commitment isn't just a static choice; it's a dynamic step toward understanding the implications of your financial choices on a personal and global scale.

Are you ready to make your mark? Begin the "Bitcoin or Death Challenge" and let it guide you through a transformative journey...

1. Choose Your Stand

Having delved into the book's depths, it's your turn to take a stand. Do you embrace Bitcoin's transformative potential, or remain within the confines of the existing system?

Reflect on your journey and make a decisive choice. Grab a pen—no pencils allowed—and mark your decision boldly within the book. This tangible act symbolizes more than a choice; it's a commitment etched into history...

Circle one:

Bitcoin	Death

If you're reading this on an eBook, circling the screen just doesn't quite do justice. Do yourself a favour and indulge in the physical copy too! If you've journeyed this far, the commitment aspect alone is priceless. Visit BitcoinOrDeath.com to secure your copy and solidify your commitment.

2. Share the Dilemma

Having etched your bold decision into the sacred pages of "Bitcoin or Death," it's time to unveil it to the world. This step goes beyond re-affirming your stance; it's about embracing the responsibility to follow through with your choice.

Moreover, as you share your personal declaration, it sets in motion a ripple effect that extends far beyond yourself.

Sharing your stance isn't just a gesture of goodwill; it's a duty you must undertake. Posing the question and sharing the book is like throwing a rope over the prison wall you've just scaled—extending a lifeline to help those you love escape the confines of the current system that enslaves them.

Your unique insights have the power to do more than spark curiosity; they can initiate conversations and inspire change. Whether you gift a copy of the book or proudly wear the exclusive "Bitcoin or Death" t-shirt, your actions transcend mere visual expression; they extend an invitation to others to engage in a thought-provoking conversation.

Direct purchases of books for gifts AND merch to wear, can be made at: BitcoinOrDeath.com

3. Ignite Change with #BitcoinOrDeath

Tag yourself wearing the shirt and make your voice heard. It's about getting loud, and getting the question heard! As you navigate the world, whenever you see a fiat currency issue surface — be it inflation, discussions on the cost of living, or the repercussions of global conflicts — use the hashtag #BitcoinOrDeath on social media. Bring attention to these issues and contribute to the orange pill movement.

We closely monitor the hashtag, rewarding exceptional posts periodically. So, as you scroll through your feed and encounter posts about everyday struggles fuelled by fiat, join the conversation by replying with #BitcoinOrDeath. Be a catalyst for change and fight for Bitcoin, in the face of death.

Bitcoin or Death... is it more than just a question, like how Bitcoin is more than money?

One day, I doubt I will see it becoming a mantra, a way of life. But then again, who knows? Maybe, just maybe, it has to be — for our own survival — worn on our sleeve as a tattoo, imprinted in our heart, and etched into our DNA, the human ledger of knowledge, passed down from generation to generation, as immutable and indestructible as Bitcoin itself. A forever question. Here's to wishful thinking. For now, the question is all I need; it's all you need, and it's enough.

Made in the USA
Monee, IL
05 November 2026

67381954R00085